VOL. 33

HAL•LEONARD®
GUITAR
PLAY-ALONG

AUDIO ACCESS INCLUDED

ACOUSTIC
Classics

PLAYBACK+
Speed • Pitch • Balance • Loop

To access audio visit:
www.halleonard.com/mylibrary

Enter Code
4360-4195-7204-2612

Tracking, mixing, and mastering by
Jake Johnson
All guitars by Doug Boduch
Bass by Tom McGirr
Keyboards by Warren Wiegratz
Drums by Scott Schroedl

ISBN: 978-0-634-08261-0

HAL•LEONARD®

Visit Hal Leonard Online at
www.halleonard.com

Contact Us:
Hal Leonard
7777 West Bluemound Road
Milwaukee, WI 53213
Email: info@halleonard.com

In Europe contact:
Hal Leonard Europe Limited
Distribution Centre, Newmarket Road
Bury St Edmunds, Suffolk, IP33 3YB
Email: info@halleonardeurope.com

In Australia contact:
Hal Leonard Australia Pty. Ltd.
4 Lentara Court
Cheltenham, Victoria, 3192 Australia
Email: info@halleonard.com.au

Guitar Notation Legend

THE MUSICAL STAFF shows pitches and rhythms and is divided by bar lines into measures. Pitches are named after the first seven letters of the alphabet.

TABLATURE graphically represents the guitar fingerboard. Each horizontal line represents a string, and each number represents a fret.

4th string, 2nd fret   1st & 2nd strings open, played together   open D chord

HALF-STEP BEND: Strike the note and bend up 1/2 step.

WHOLE-STEP BEND: Strike the note and bend up one step.

GRACE NOTE BEND: Strike the note and bend up as indicated. The first note does not take up any time.

SLIGHT (MICROTONE) BEND: Strike the note and bend up 1/4 step.

BEND AND RELEASE: Strike the note and bend up as indicated, then release back to the original note. Only the first note is struck.

PRE-BEND: Bend the note as indicated, then strike it.

VIBRATO: The string is vibrated by rapidly bending and releasing the note with the fretting hand.

PALM MUTING: The note is partially muted by the pick hand lightly touching the string(s) just before the bridge.

HAMMER-ON: Strike the first (lower) note with one finger, then sound the higher note (on the same string) with another finger by fretting it without picking.

PULL-OFF: Place both fingers on the notes to be sounded. Strike the first note and without picking, pull the finger off to sound the second (lower) note.

LEGATO SLIDE: Strike the first note and then slide the same fret-hand finger up or down to the second note. The second note is not struck.

SHIFT SLIDE: Same as legato slide, except the second note is struck.

TRILL: Very rapidly alternate between the notes indicated by continuously hammering on and pulling off.

TAPPING: Hammer ("tap") the fret indicated with the pick-hand index or middle finger and pull off to the note fretted by the fret hand.

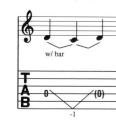

NATURAL HARMONIC: Strike the note while the fret-hand lightly touches the string directly over the fret indicated.

PINCH HARMONIC: The note is fretted normally and a harmonic is produced by adding the edge of the thumb or the tip of the index finger of the pick hand to the normal pick attack.

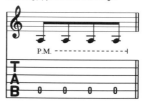

TREMOLO PICKING: The note is picked as rapidly and continuously as possible.

VIBRATO BAR DIVE AND RETURN: The pitch of the note or chord is dropped a specified number of steps (in rhythm) then returned to the original pitch.

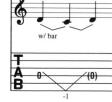

VIBRATO BAR SCOOP: Depress the bar just before striking the note, then quickly release the bar.

VIBRATO BAR DIP: Strike the note and then immediately drop a specified number of steps, then release back to the original pitch.

Additional Musical Definitions

 (accent)   • Accentuate note (play it louder)

(staccato)   • Play the note short

D.S. al Coda   • Go back to the sign (𝄋), then play until the measure marked *"To Coda"*, then skip to the section labelled *"Coda."*

D.C. al Fine   • Go back to the beginning of the song and play until the measure marked *"Fine"* (end).

Fill   • Label used to identify a brief melodic figure which is to be inserted into the arrangement.

N.C.   • Instrument is silent (drops out).

• Repeat measures between signs.

   • When a repeated section has different endings, play the first ending only the first time and the second ending only the second time.

HAL•LEONARD® GUITAR PLAY-ALONG

AUDIO ACCESS INCLUDED

VOL. 33

ACOUSTIC *Classics*

Across the Universe

Words and Music by John Lennon and Paul McCartney

Tune down 1/2 step:
(low to high) E♭-A♭-D♭-G♭-B♭-E♭

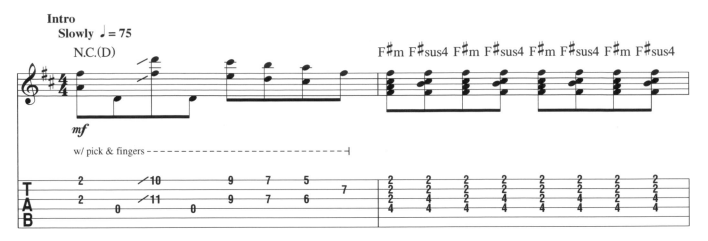

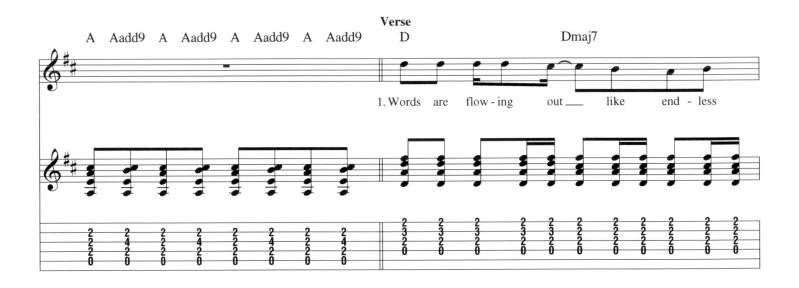

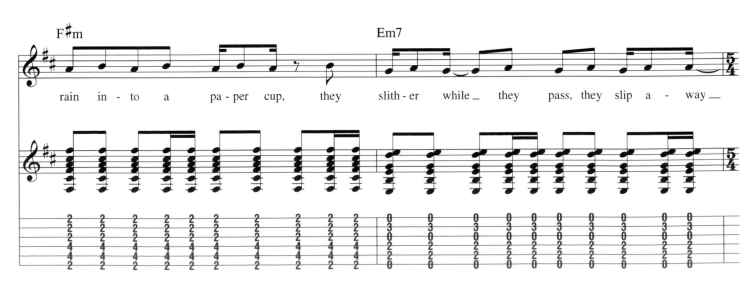

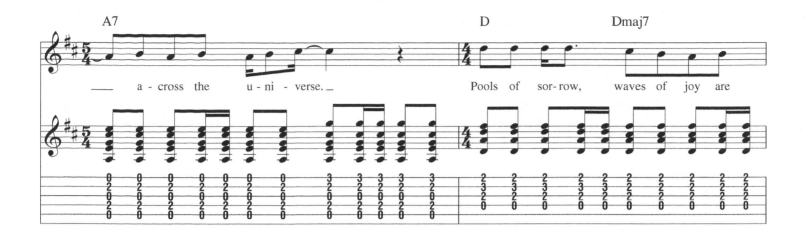

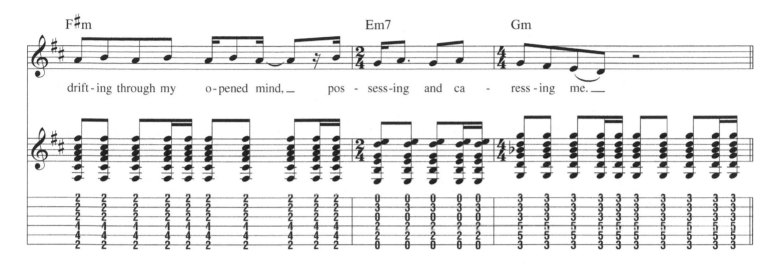

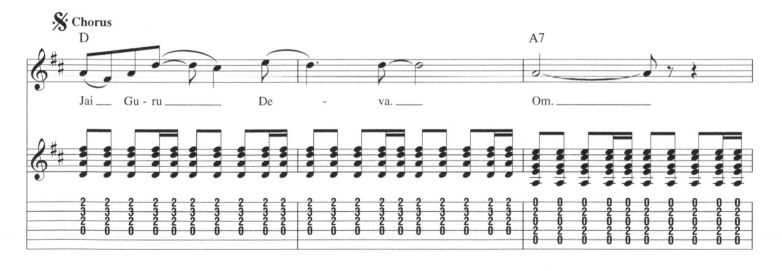

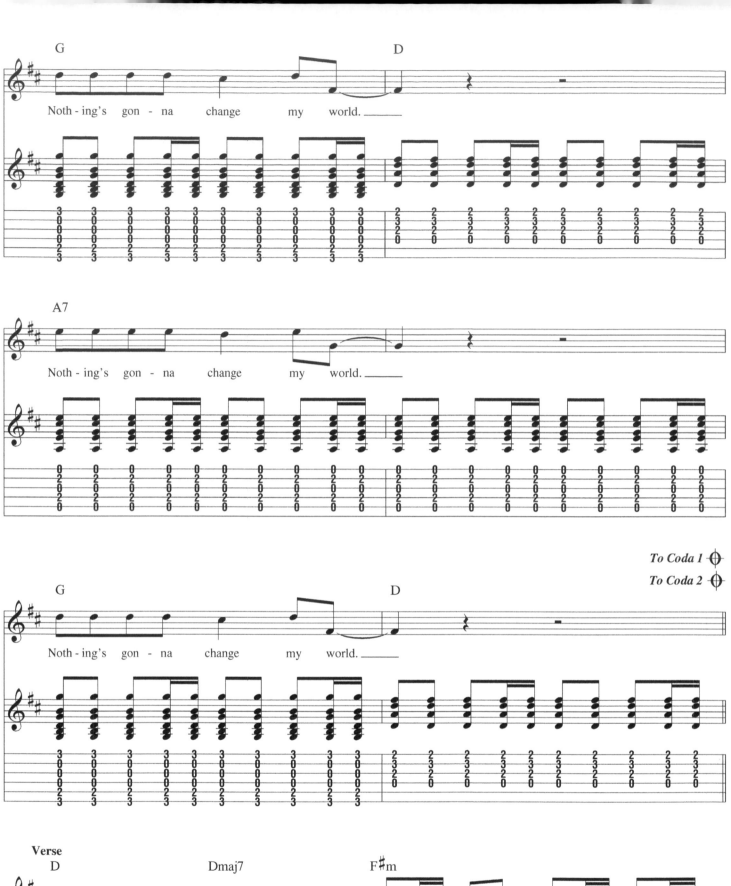

G ... *D*

Noth - ing's gon - na change my world. _____

A7

Noth - ing's gon - na change my world. _____

To Coda 1 ⊕
To Coda 2 ⊕

G ... *D*

Noth - ing's gon - na change my world. _____

Verse

D ... *Dmaj7* ... *F#m*

2. Im - ag - es _____ of bro - ken light which dance be - fore _____ me like a mil - lion eyes, _____

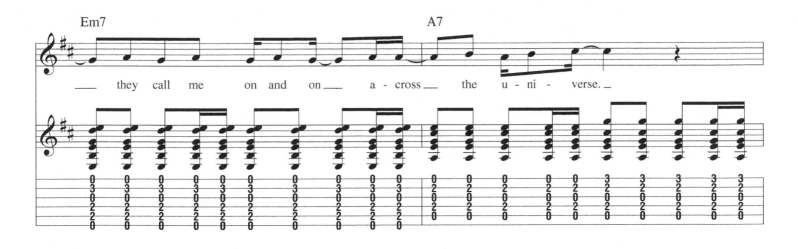

they call me on and on _ a-cross _ the u - ni - verse. _

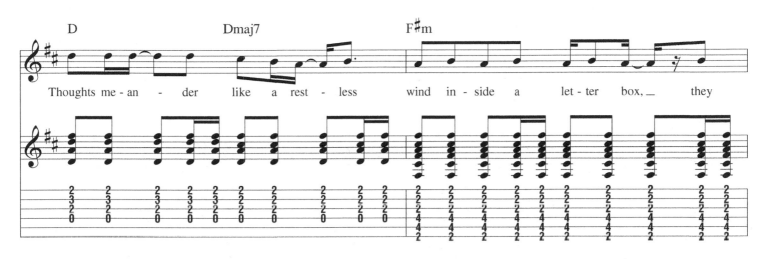

Thoughts me - an - der like a rest - less wind in - side a let - ter box, _ they

D.S. al Coda 1

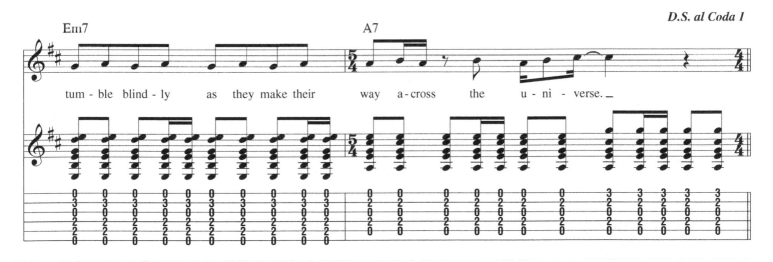

tum - ble blind - ly as they make their way a - cross the u - ni - verse. _

Coda 1

Verse

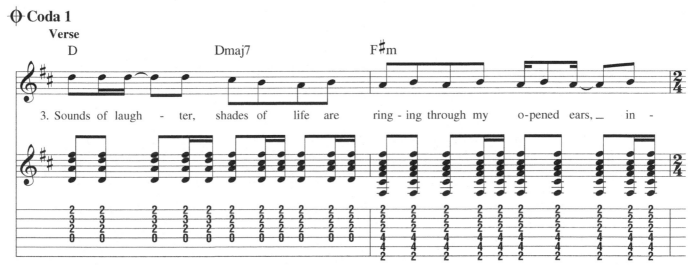

3. Sounds of laugh - ter, shades of life are ring - ing through my o-pened ears, _ in -

Babe, I'm Gonna Leave You

Words and Music by Anne Bredon, Jimmy Page and Robert Plant

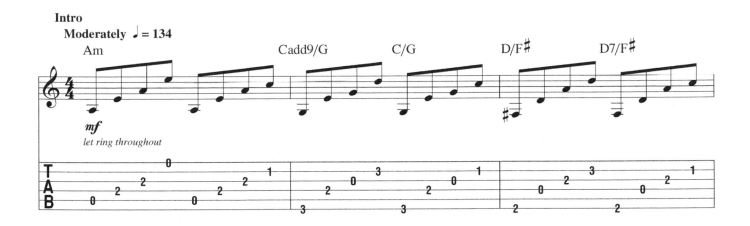

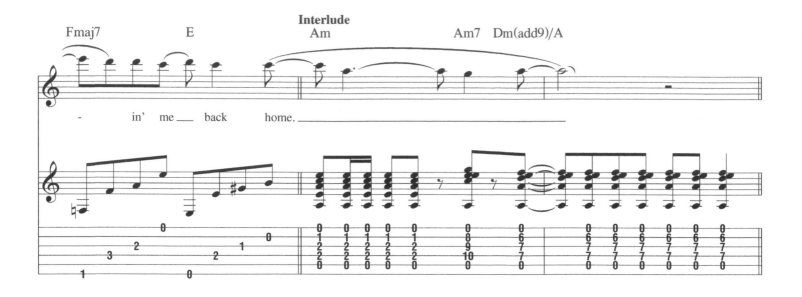

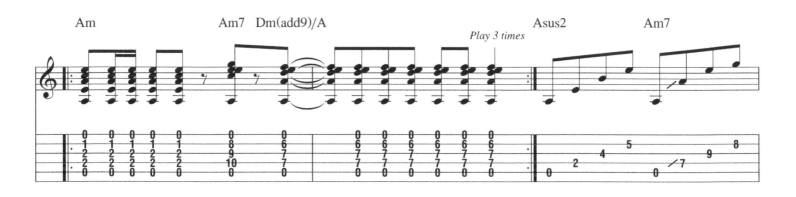

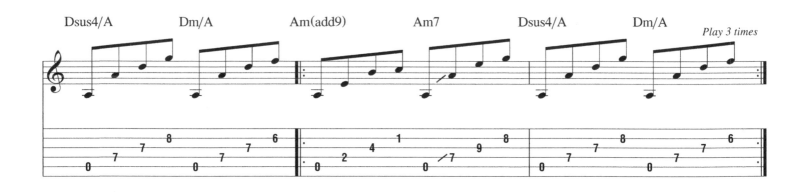

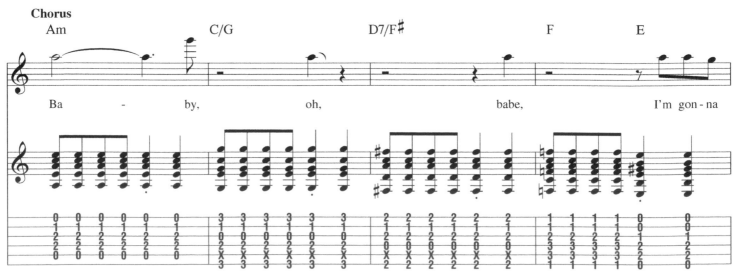

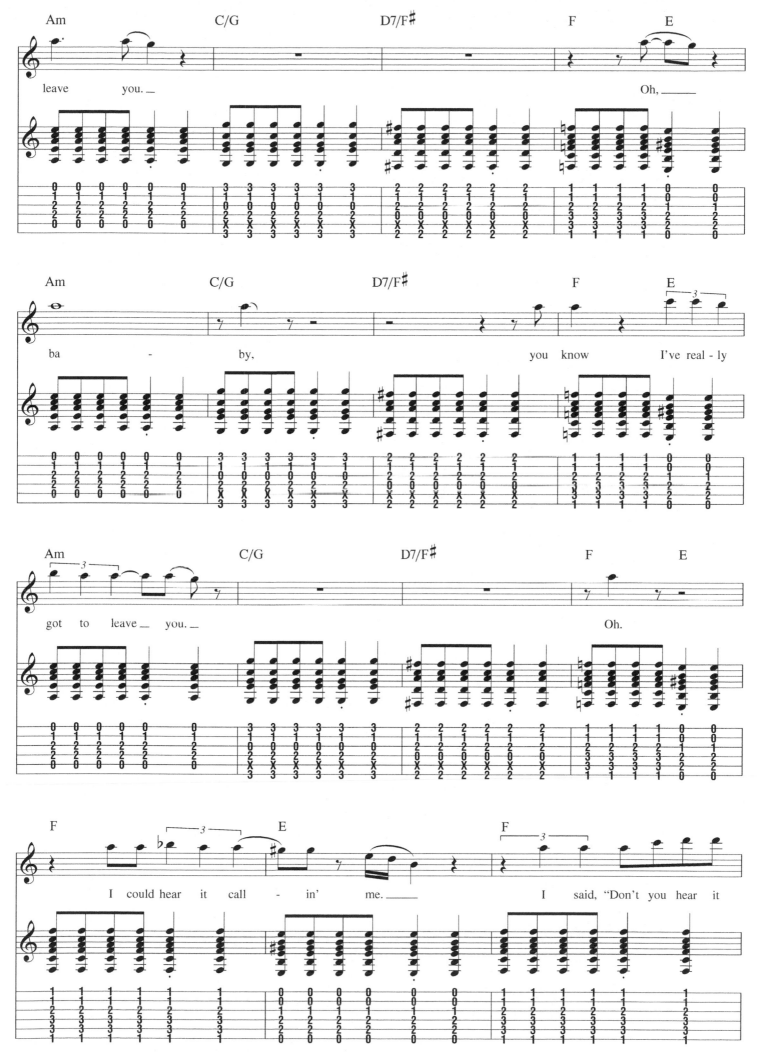

Interlude

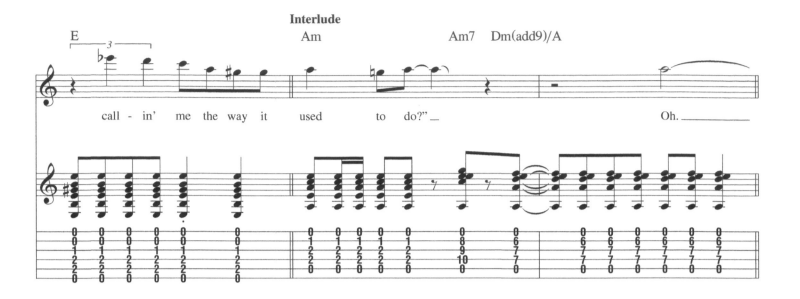

call - in' me the way it used to do?" _____ Oh. _____

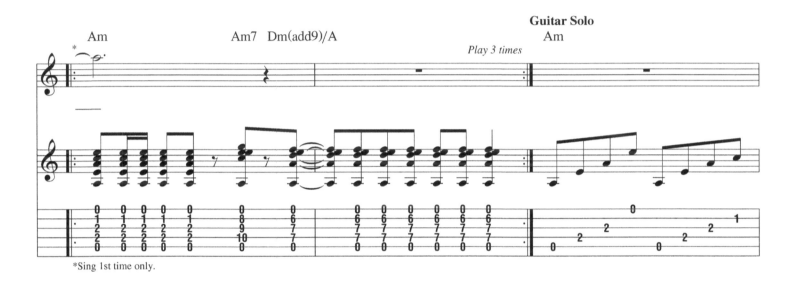

*Sing 1st time only.

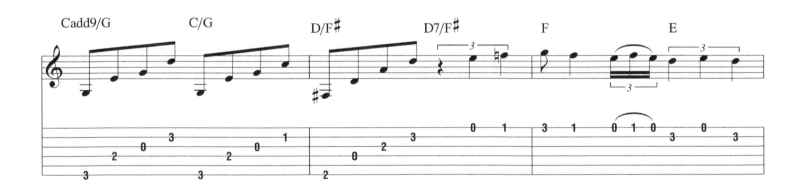

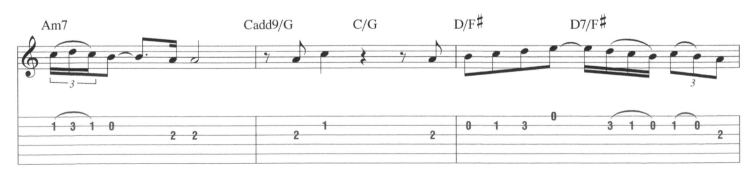

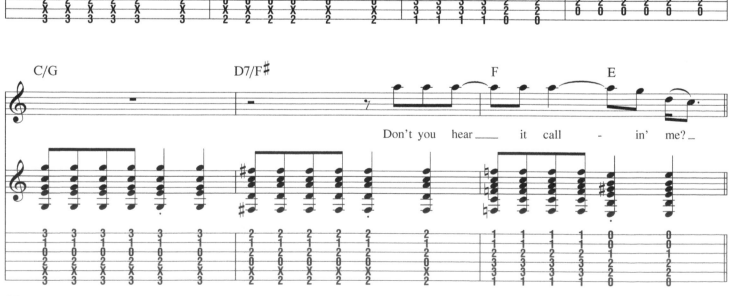

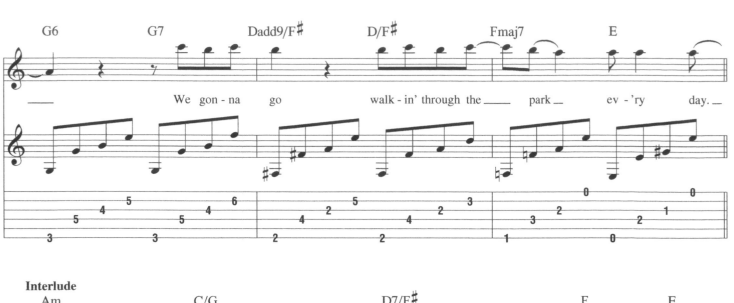

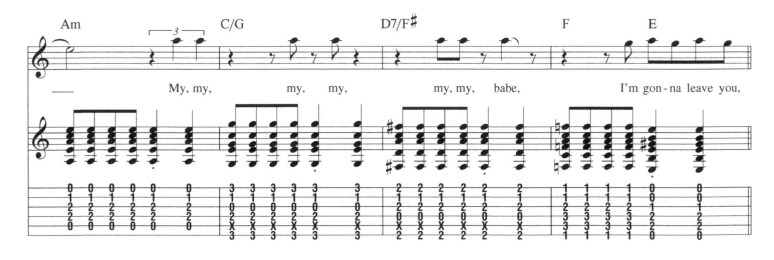

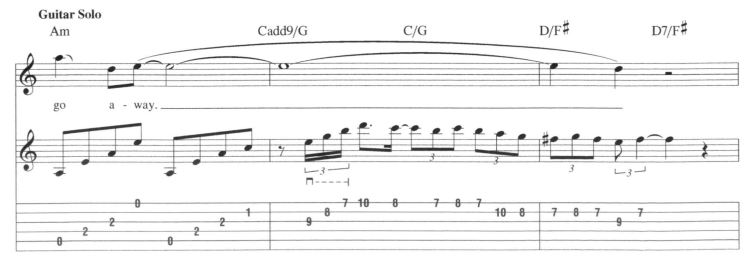

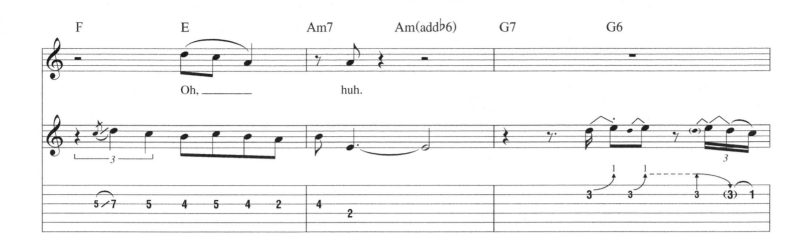

Oh, _____ huh.

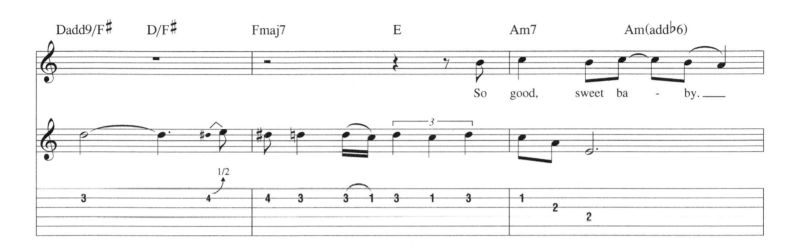

So good, sweet ba - by. _____

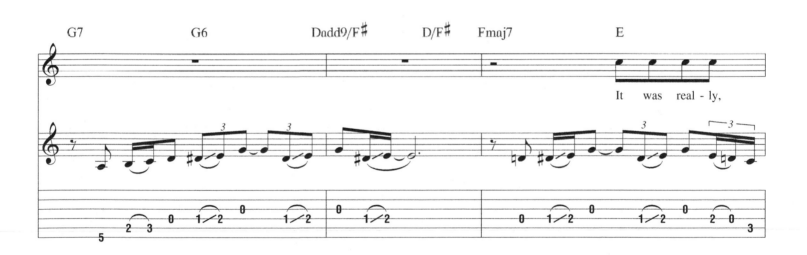

It was real - ly,

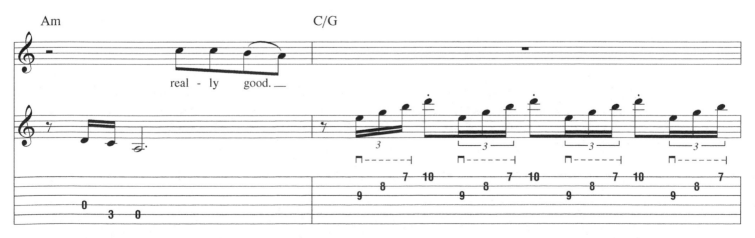

real - ly good. _____

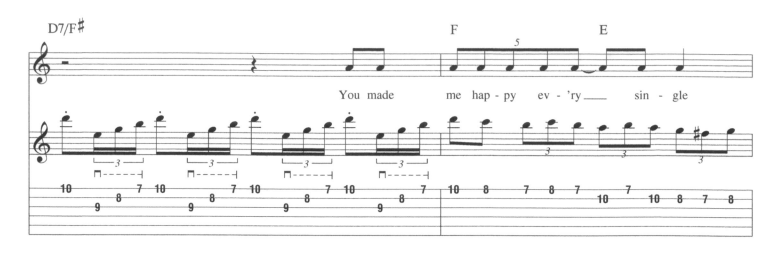

You made me hap-py ev-'ry____ sin-gle

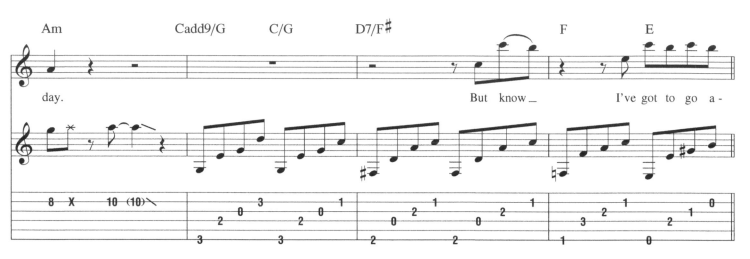

day. But know __ I've got to go a-

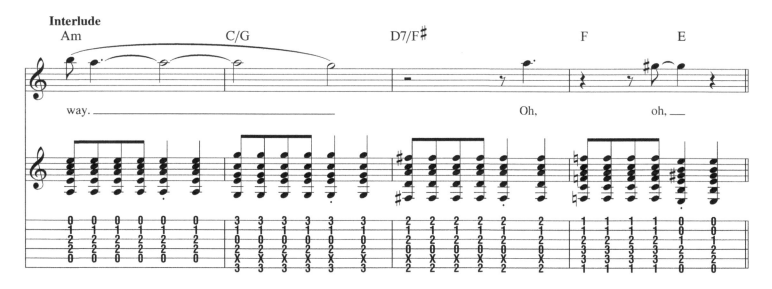

Interlude

way. _____ Oh, oh, __

w/ Voc. ad lib. on repeats

Play 3 times

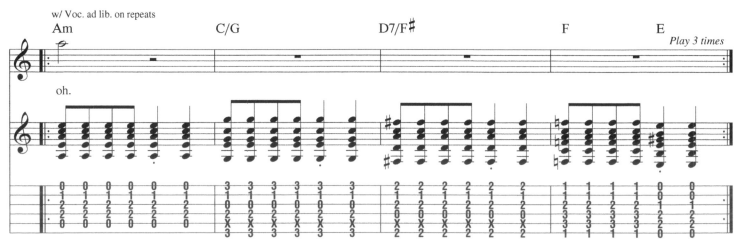

oh.

Crazy on You

Words and Music by Ann Wilson, Nancy Wilson and Roger Fisher

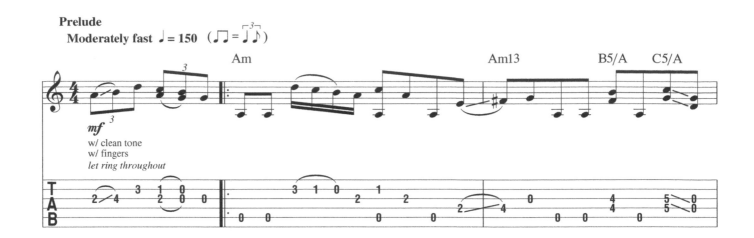

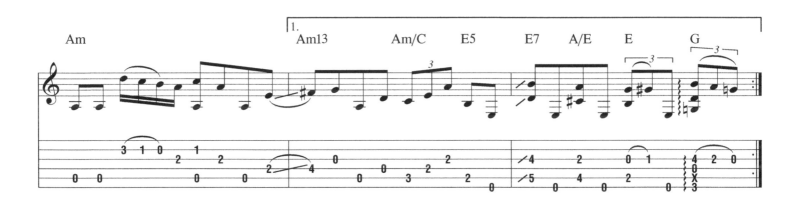

*Played as even eighth notes.

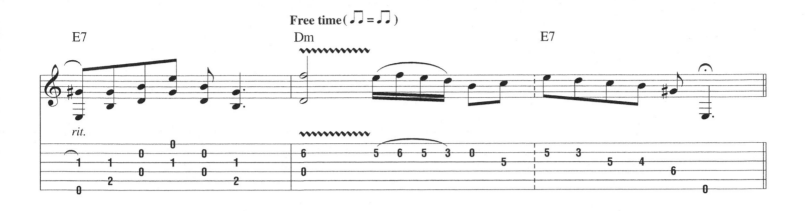

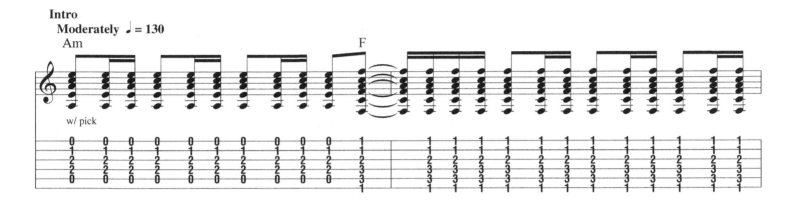

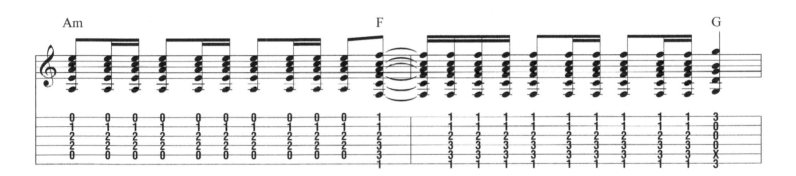

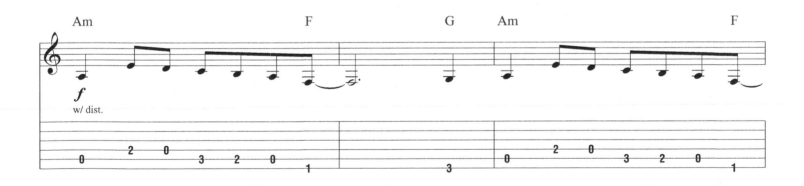

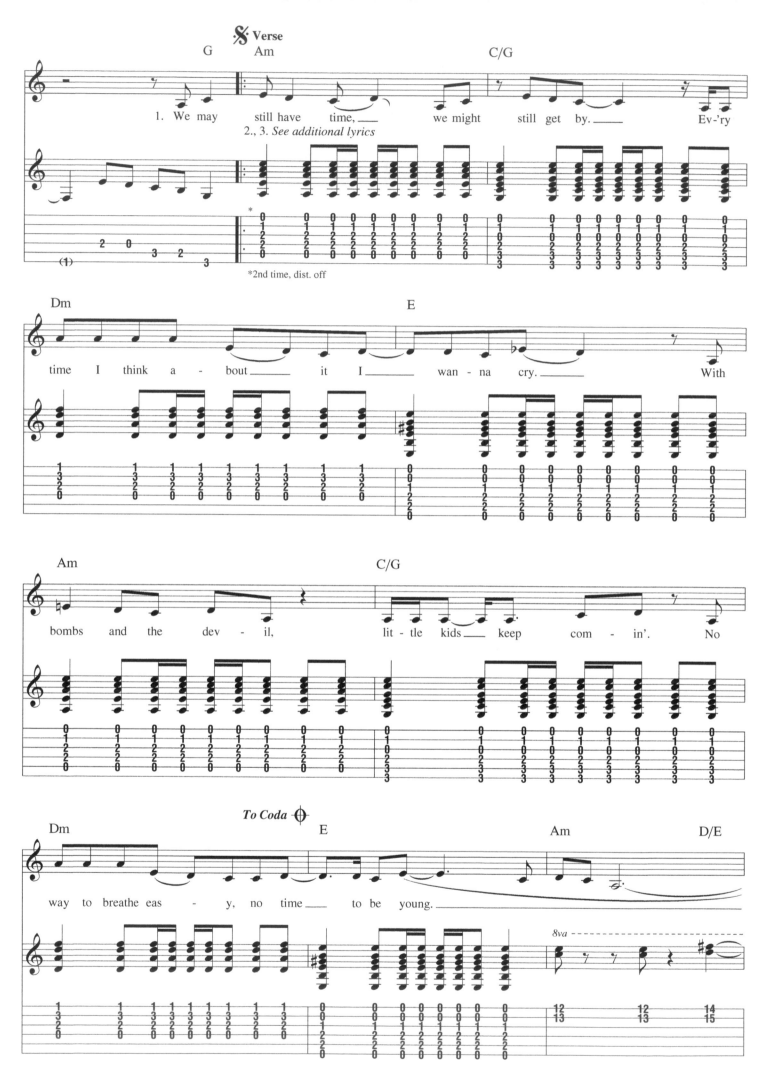

Verse

G   Am   C/G

1. We may still have time, ___ we might still get by. ___ Ev-'ry

2., 3. *See additional lyrics*

*2nd time, dist. off

Dm   E

time I think a - bout ___ it I ___ wan - na cry. ___ With

Am   C/G

bombs and the dev - il, lit - tle kids ___ keep com - in'. No

To Coda ⊕

Dm   E   Am   D/E

way to breathe eas - y, no time ___ to be young. _____

8va

26

Pre-Chorus

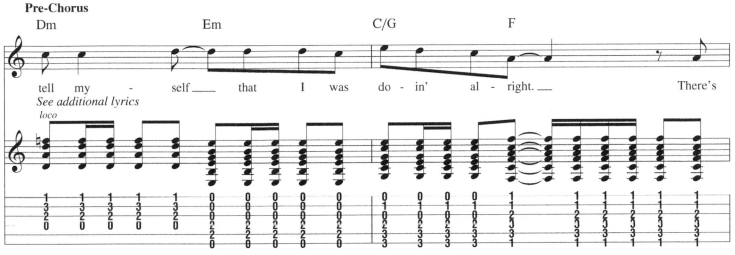

tell my-self ___ that I was do-in' al-right. ___ There's
See additional lyrics

Chorus

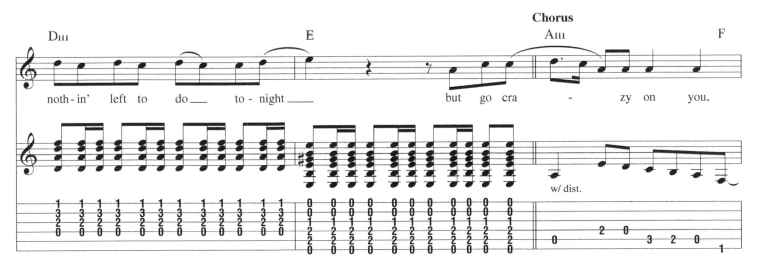

noth-in' left to do ___ to-night ___ but go cra - zy on you,

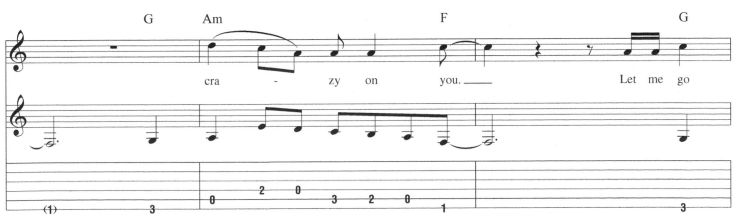

cra - zy on you. ___ Let me go

cra - zy, cra - zy on you, _____ oh. _____ 2. My

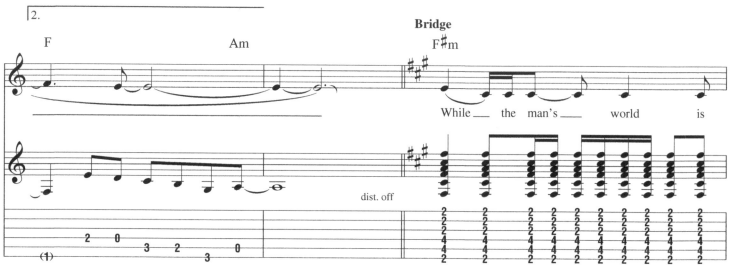

While ___ the man's ___ world is

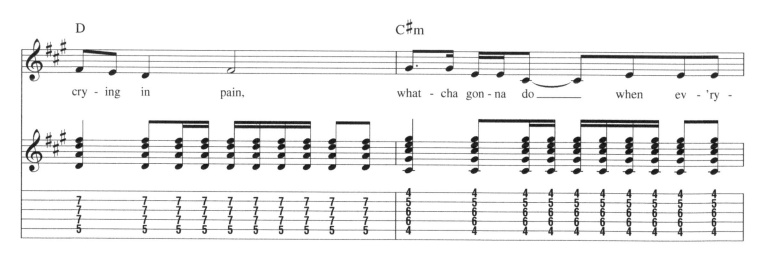

cry - ing in pain, what - cha gon - na do _____ when ev - 'ry -

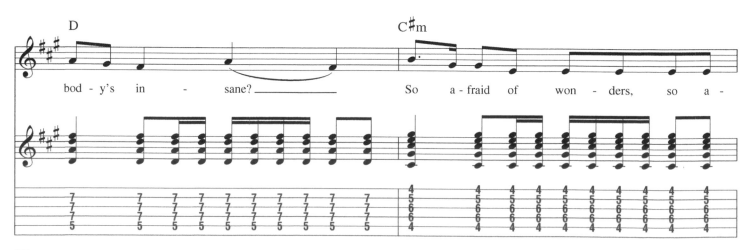

bod - y's in - sane? _____ So a - fraid of won - ders, so a -

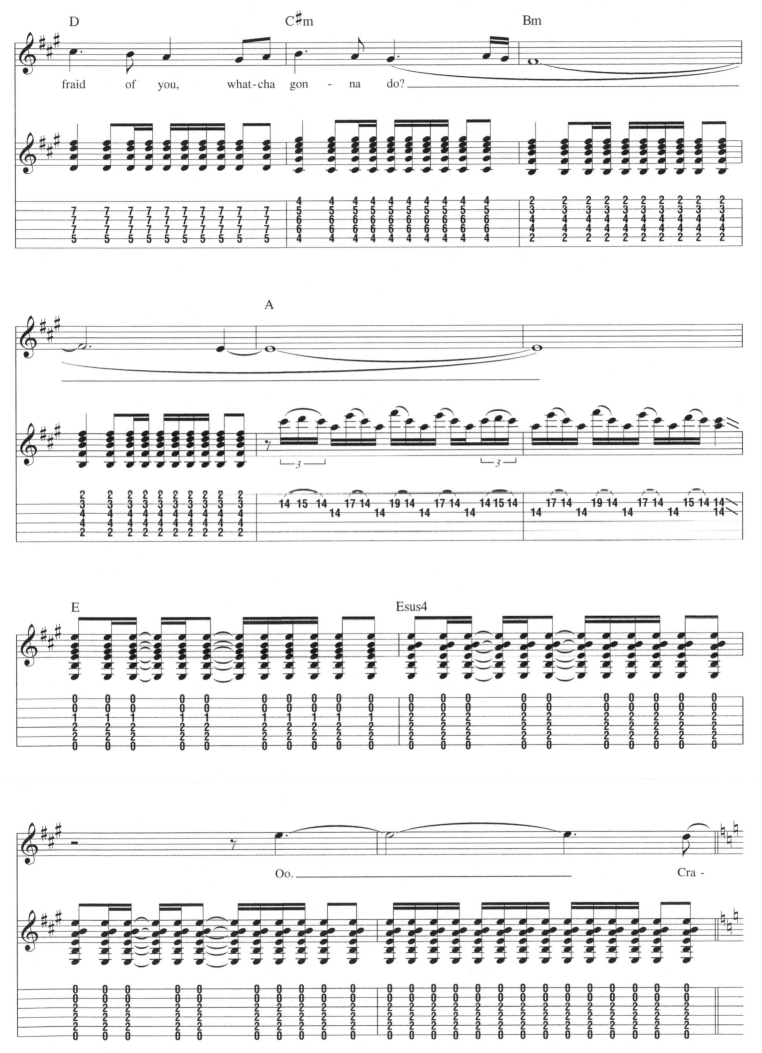

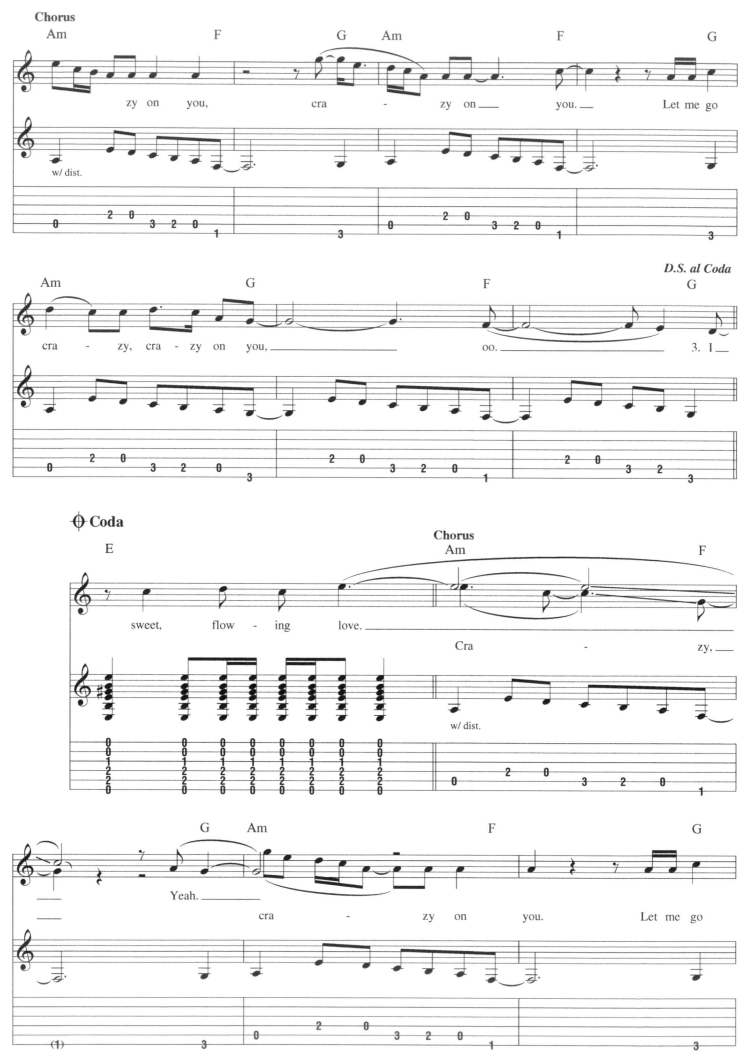

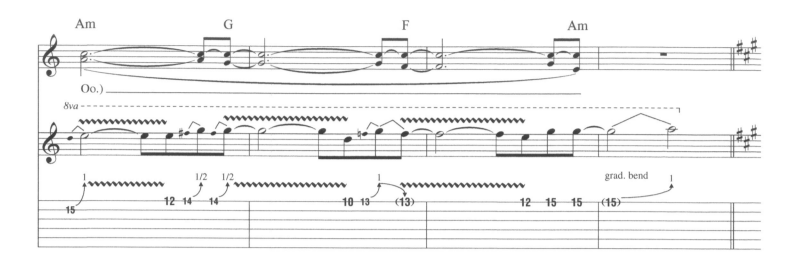

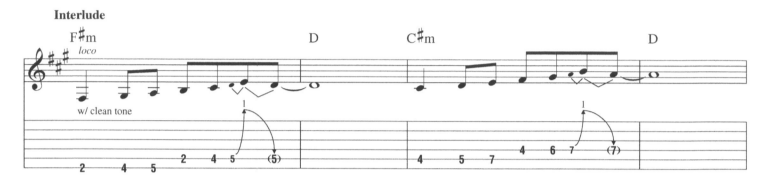

Interlude

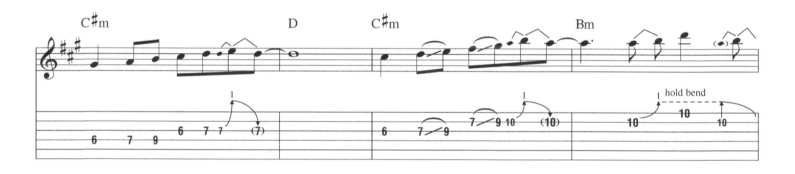

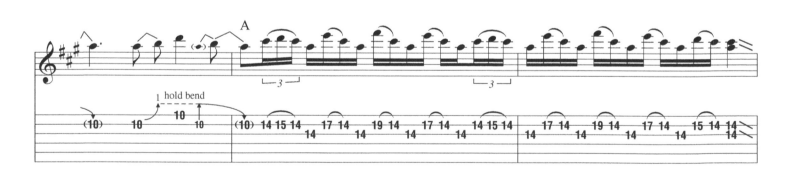

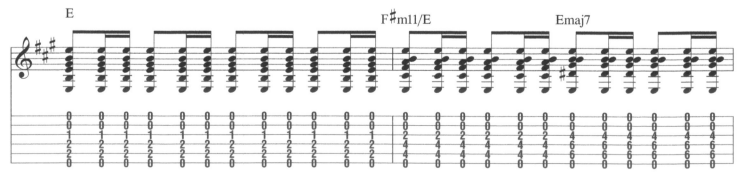

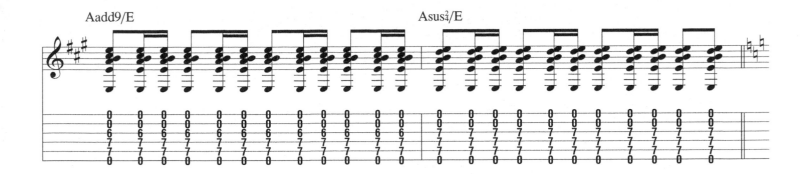

Additional Lyrics

2. My love is the evening breeze touching your skin,
   The gentle, sweet singing of leaves in the wind.
   The whisper that calls after you in the night
   And kisses your ear in the early light.

Pre-Chorus And you don't need to wonder; you're doin' fine.
   My love, the pleasure's mine.

3. I was a willow last night in a dream,
   I bent down over a clear running stream.
   I sang you this song that I heard up above
   And you kept me alive with your sweet, flowing love.

Heart of Gold

Words and Music by Neil Young

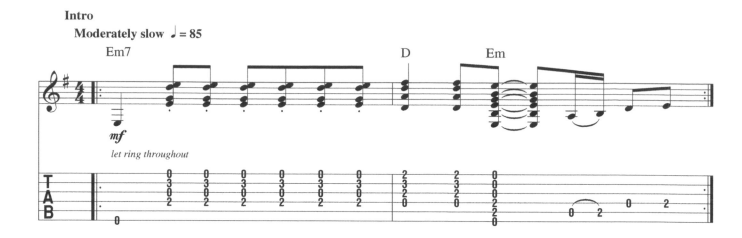

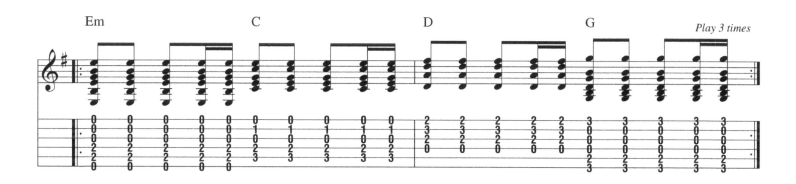

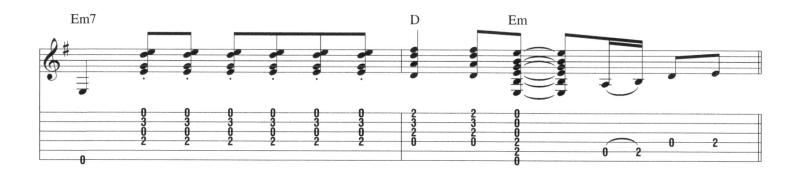

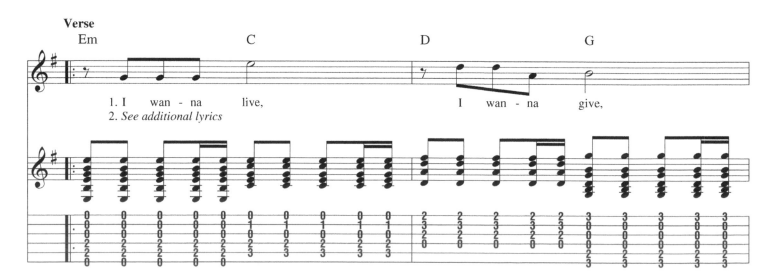

1. I wan - na live, I wan - na give,
2. *See additional lyrics*

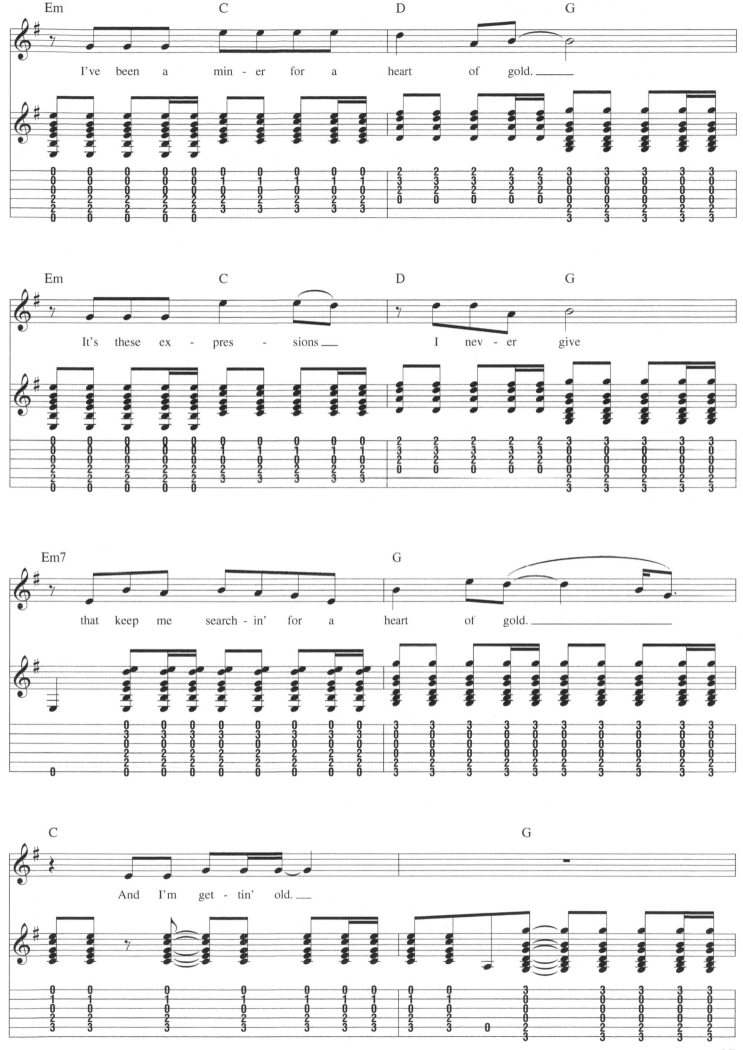

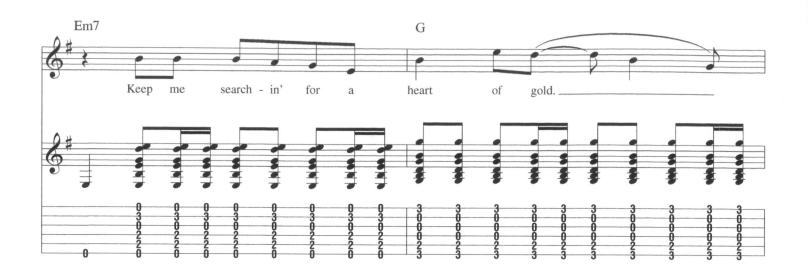

Keep me search - in' for a heart of gold.

And I'm get - tin' old. ___

Interlude

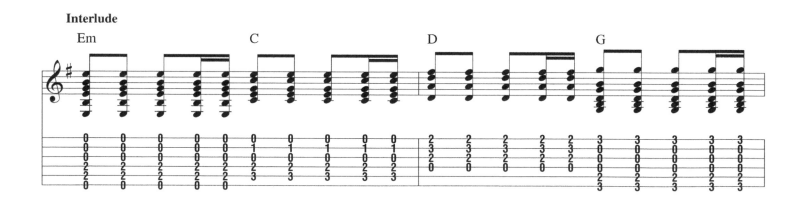

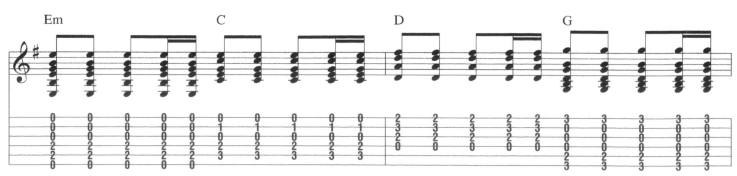

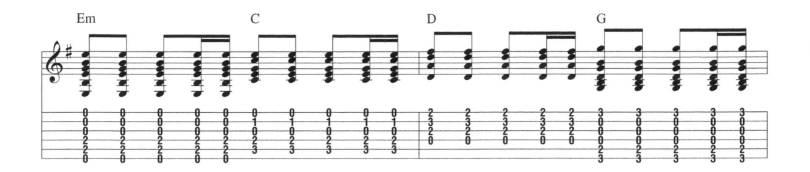

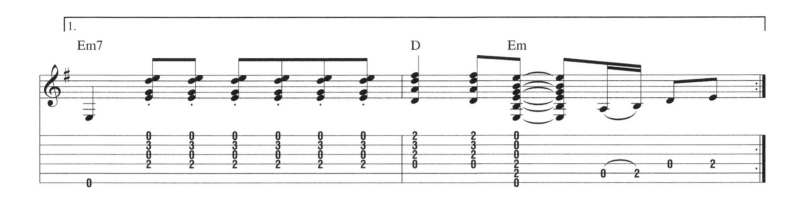

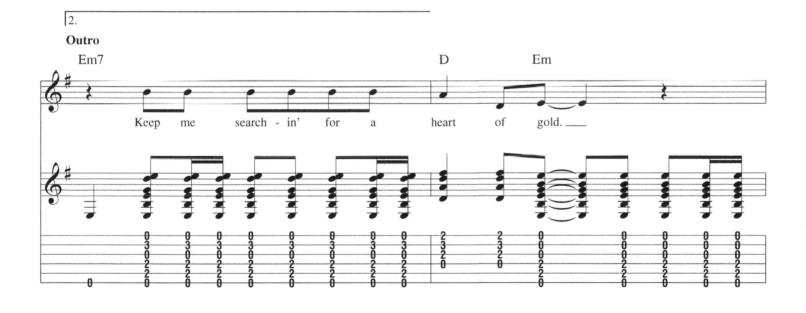

Keep me search - in' for a heart of gold. ____

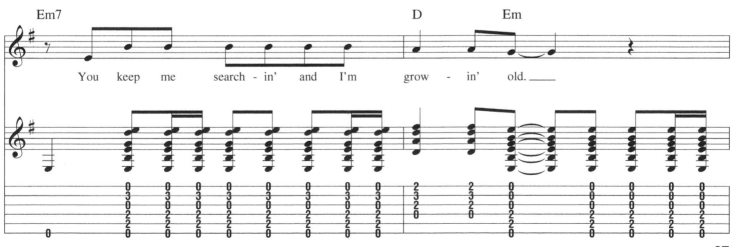

You keep me search - in' and I'm grow - in' old. ____

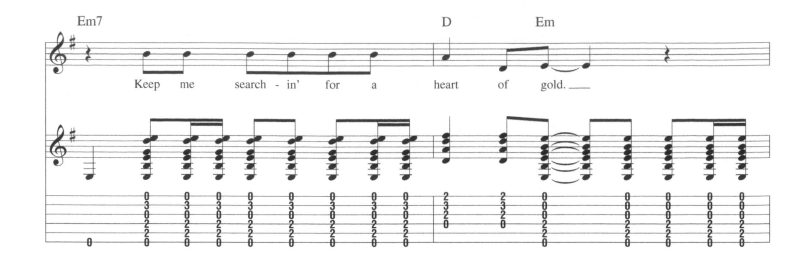

Keep me search - in' for a heart of gold. ____

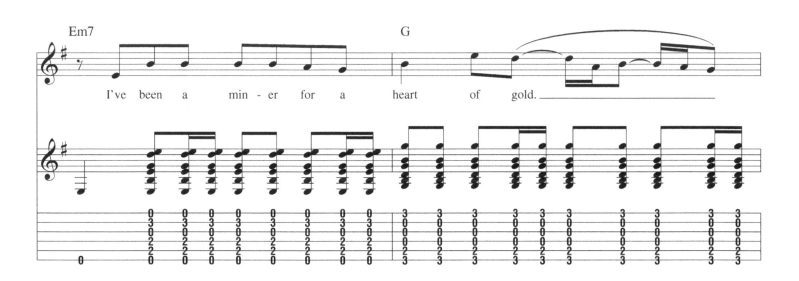

I've been a min - er for a heart of gold. ____

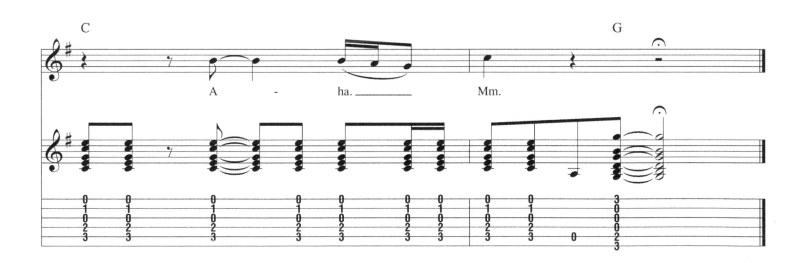

A - ha. _____ Mm.

Additional Lyrics

2. I've been to Hollywood,
   I've been to Redwood,
   I'd cross the ocean for a heart of gold.
   I've been in my mind, it's such a fine line
   That keeps me searchin' for a heart of gold.
   And I'm gettin' old.
   Keeps me searchin' for a heart of gold.
   And I'm gettin' old.

I'd Love to Change the World

Words and Music by Alvin Lee

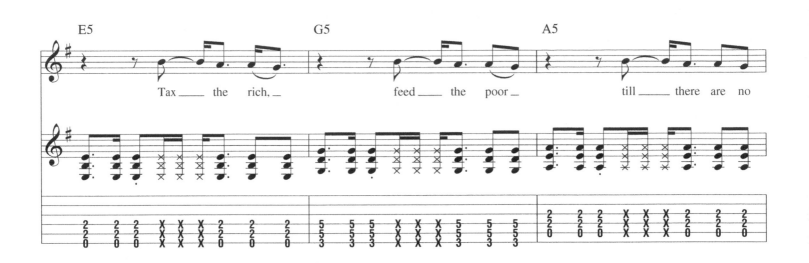

Tax ____ the rich, ____ feed ____ the poor ____ till ____ there are no

rich ____ no more. ____

𝄋 Chorus

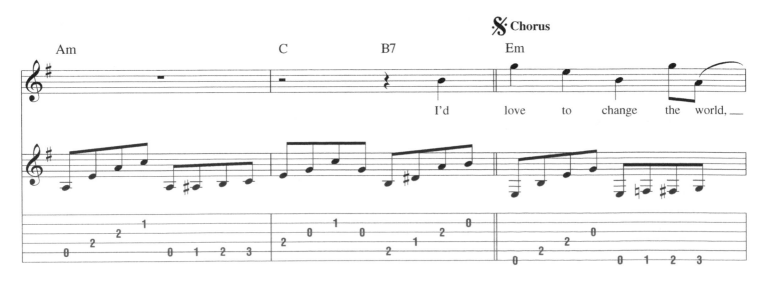

I'd love to change the world, ___

stop the war. ___

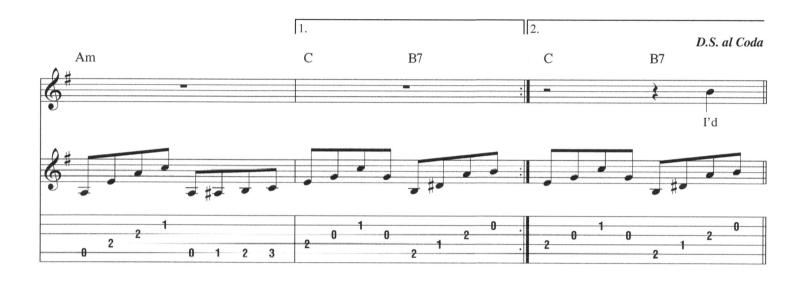

D.S. al Coda

I'd

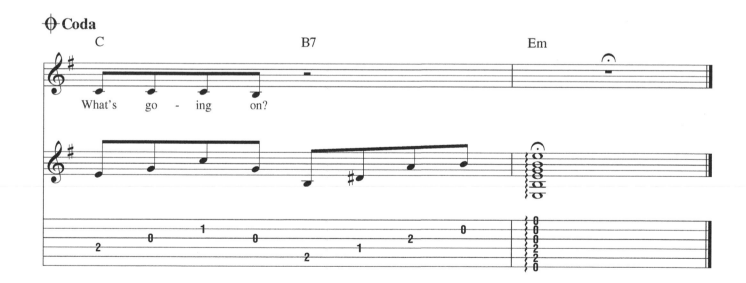

What's go - ing on?

Additional Lyrics

2. Population keeps on breeding.
   Nation bleeding, still more feeding economy.
   Life is funny; skies are sunny.
   Bees make honey; who needs money?
   Monopoly.
   No, not for me.

Hotel California

Words and Music by Don Henley, Glenn Frey and Don Felder

*Acous. gtrs. Capo VII on original recording.

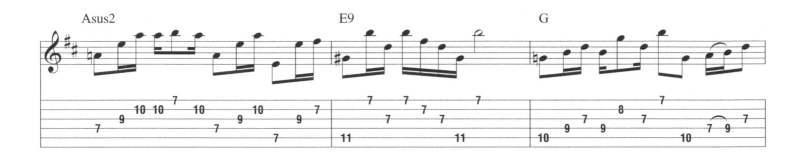

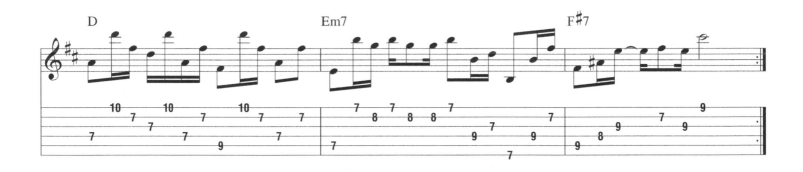

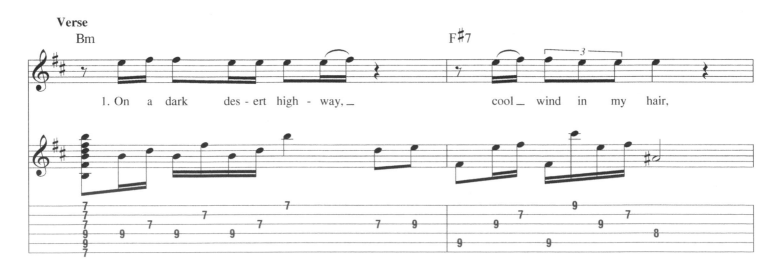

1. On a dark desert high-way, — cool — wind in my hair,

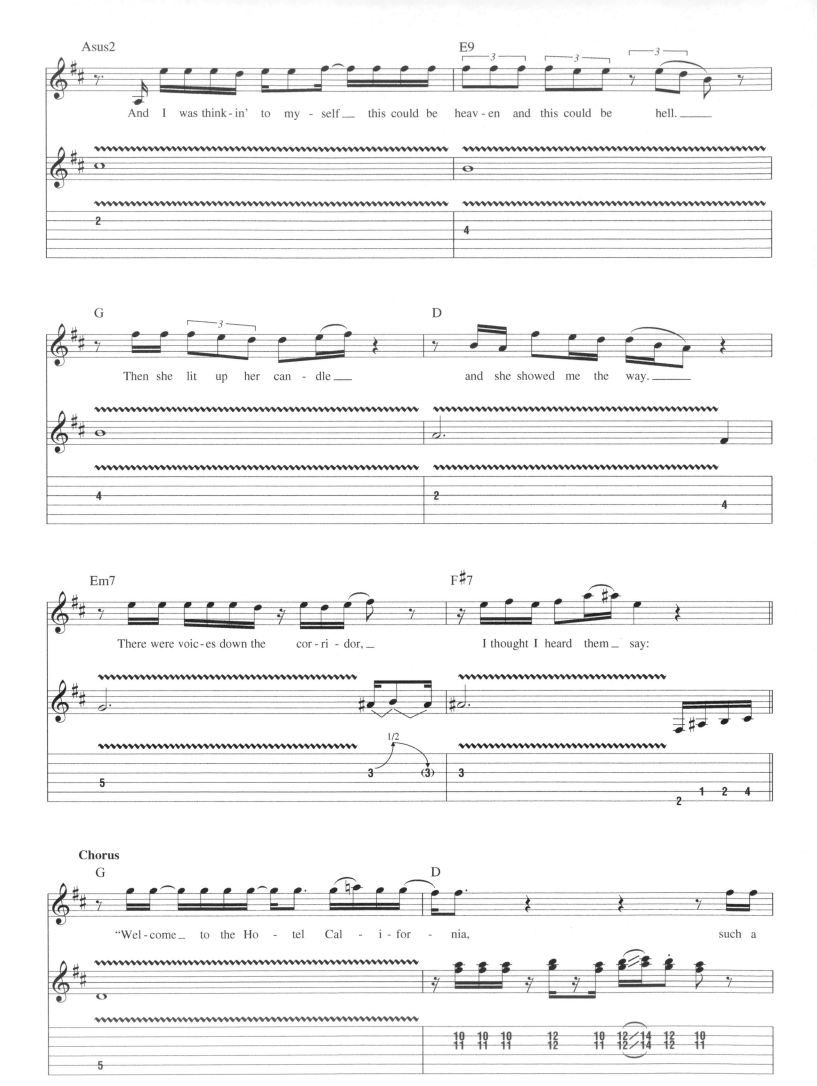

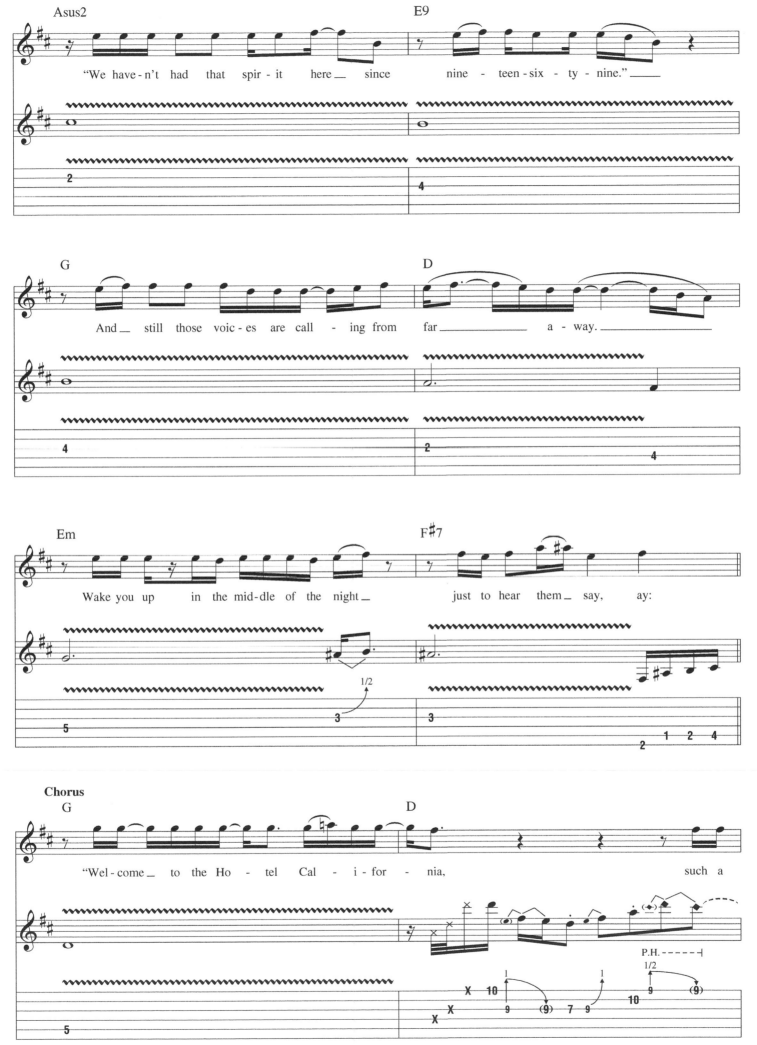

love - ly place, ____ (Such a love - ly place.) ____ such a love - ly face. ____ They're

liv - in' it up at the Ho - tel Cal - i - for - nia. What a

nice __ sur - prise. ____ (What a nice __ sur - prise.) ____ Bring your al - i - bis." ____

Verse

5. Mir - rors __ on the ceil - ing, __ the pink cham - pagne on ice, __ And she said,

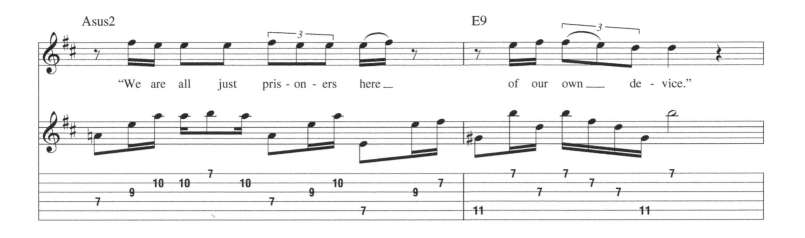

"We are all just pris - on - ers here __ of our own __ de - vice."

And in the __ mas - ter's cham - bers __ they gath - ered for the feast.

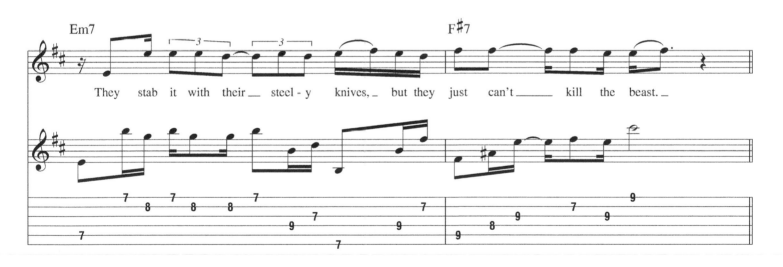

They stab it with their __ steel - y knives, __ but they just can't __ kill the beast. __

Verse

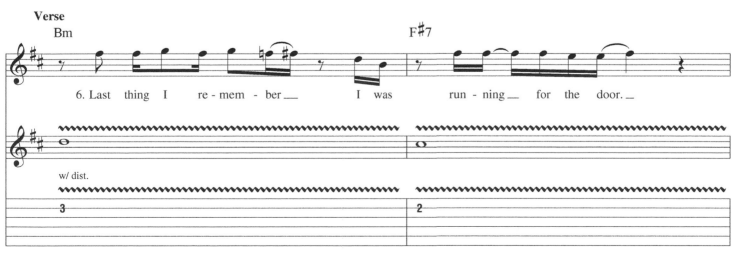

6. Last thing I re - mem - ber __ I was run - ning __ for the door. __

w/ dist.

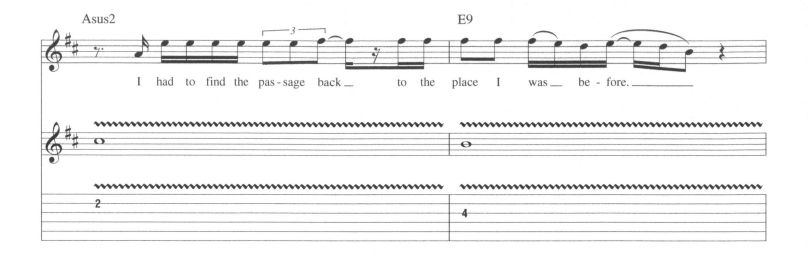

I had to find the pas-sage back __ to the place I was __ be-fore. __

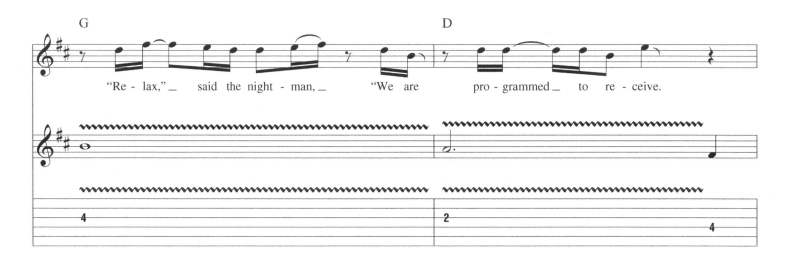

"Re - lax," __ said the night - man, __ "We are pro-grammed __ to re - ceive.

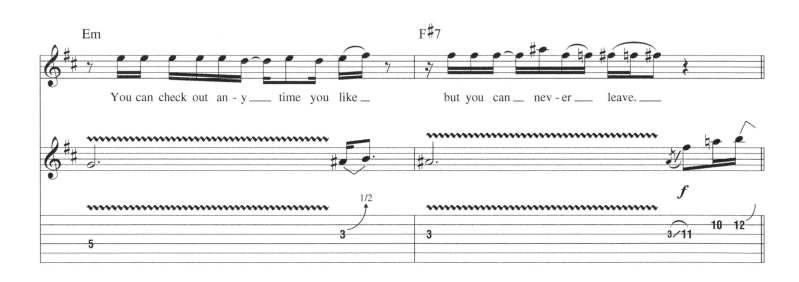

You can check out an - y __ time you like __ but you can __ nev - er __ leave. __

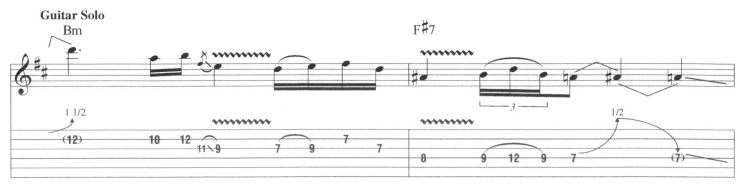

Guitar Solo

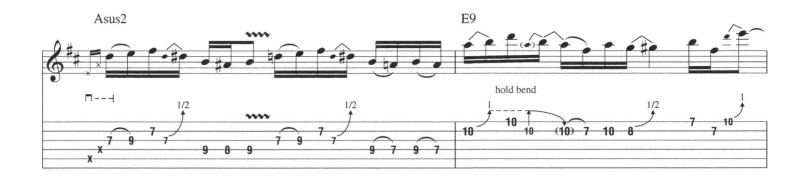

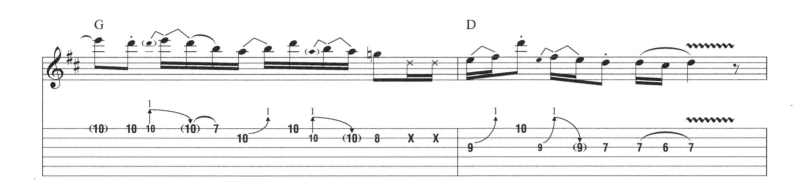

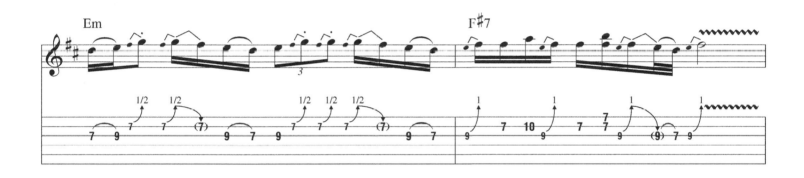

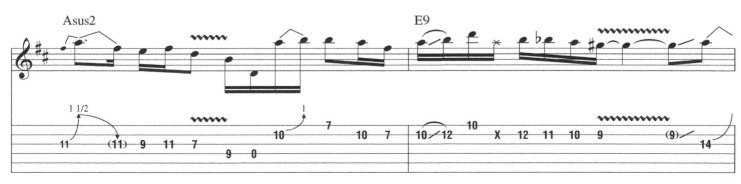

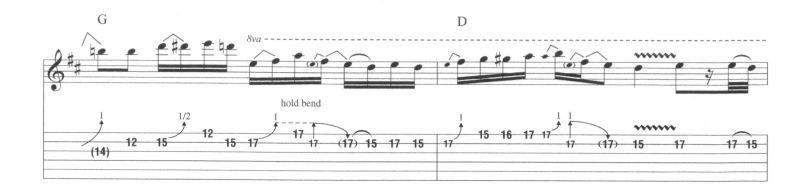

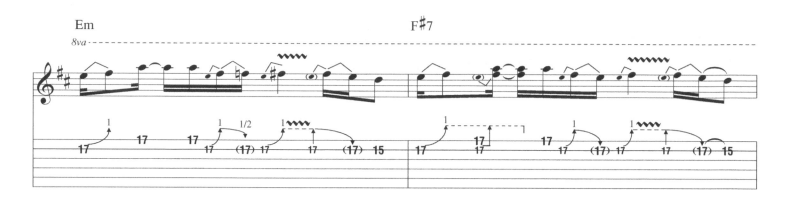

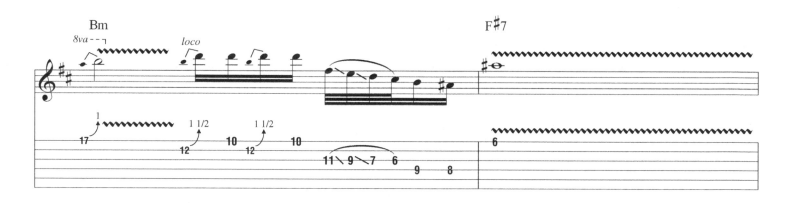

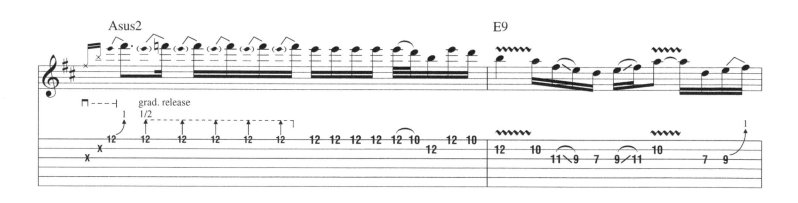

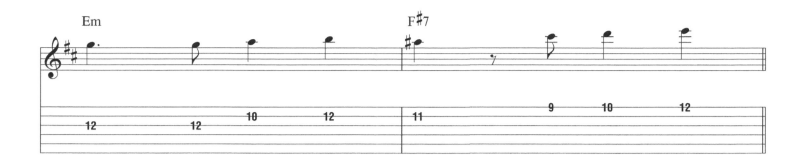

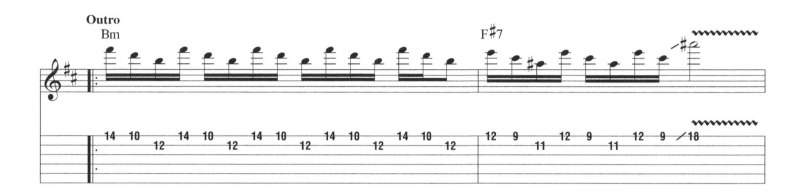

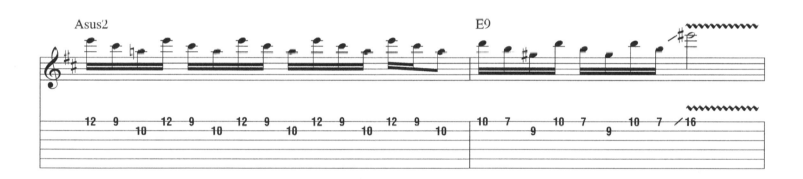

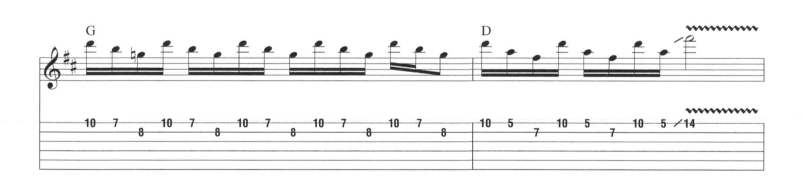

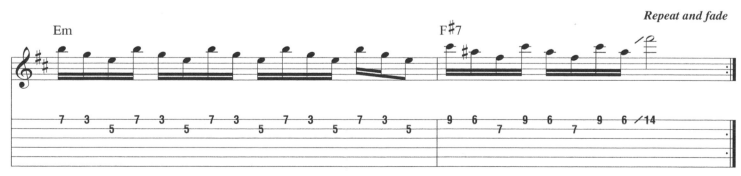

Thick as a Brick

Words and Music by Ian Anderson

Capo III

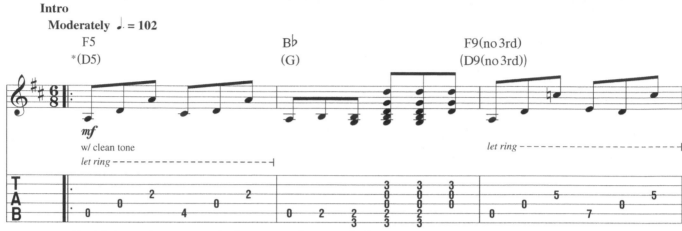

*Symbols in parentheses represent chord names respective to capoed guitar.
Symbols above reflect actual sounding chords. Capoed fret is "0" in tab.

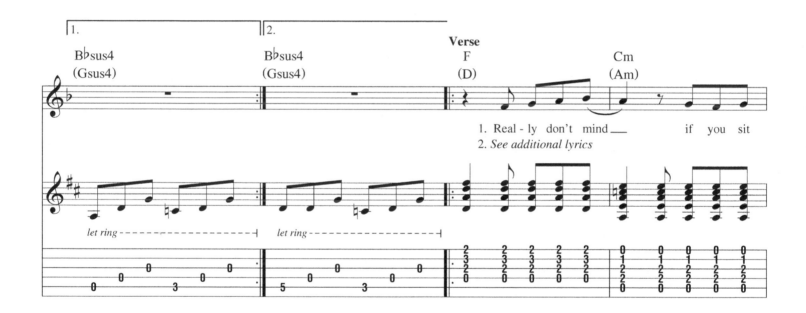

1. Real - ly don't mind ___ if you sit
2. *See additional lyrics*

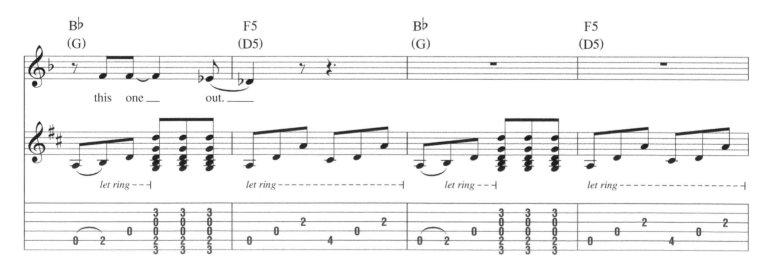

this one ___ out. ___

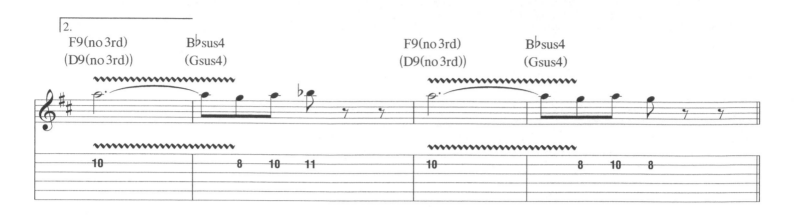

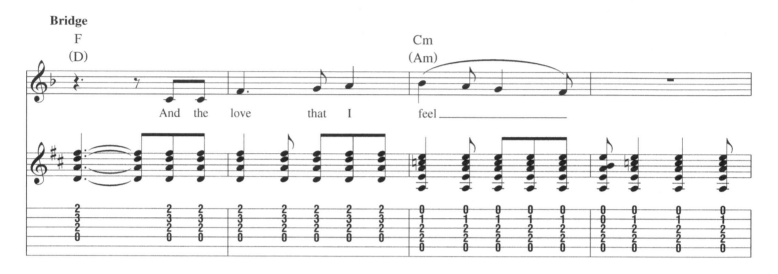

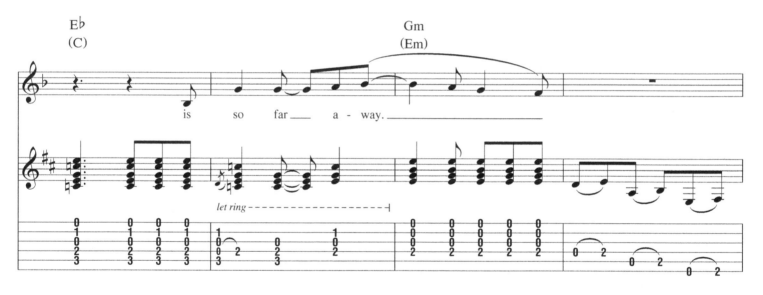

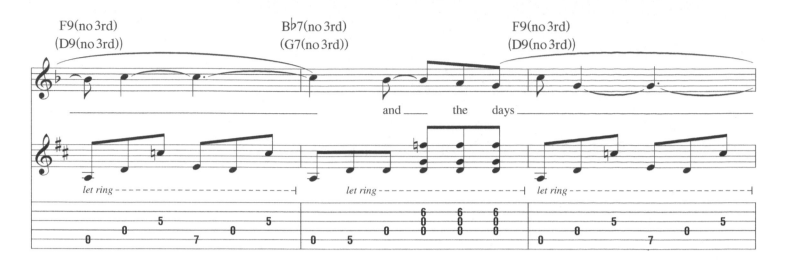

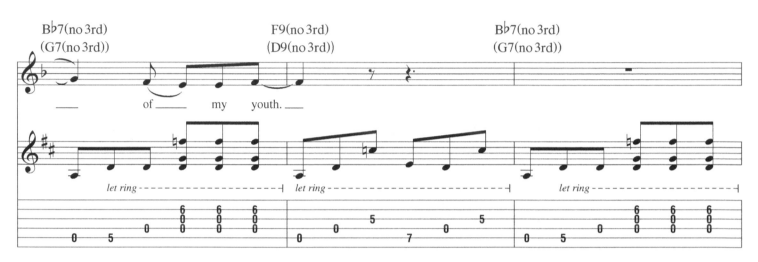

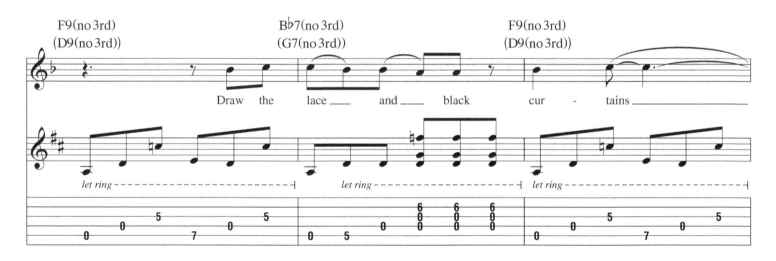

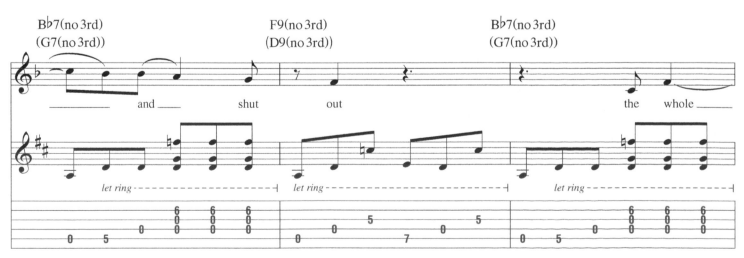

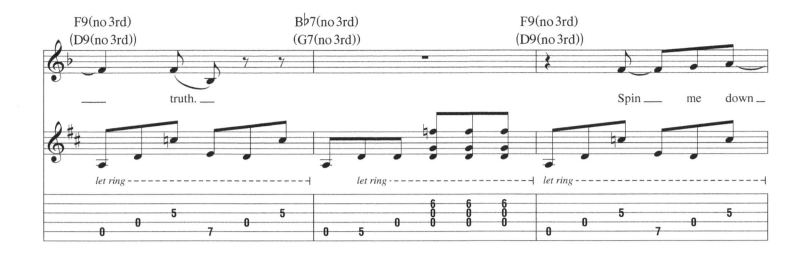

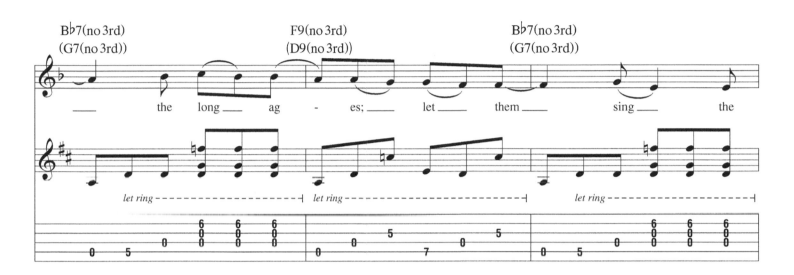

Additional Lyrics

2. And the sand castle virtues are all swept away
In the tidal destruction, the moral melee.
The elastic retreat rings the close of play
As the last wave uncovers the newfangled way.

Chorus But your new shoes are worn at the heels,
And your suntan does rapidly peel,
And your wise men don't know how it feels
To be thick as a brick.

Wanted Dead or Alive

Words and Music by Jon Bon Jovi and Richie Sambora

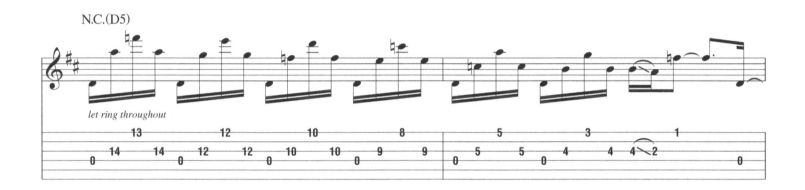

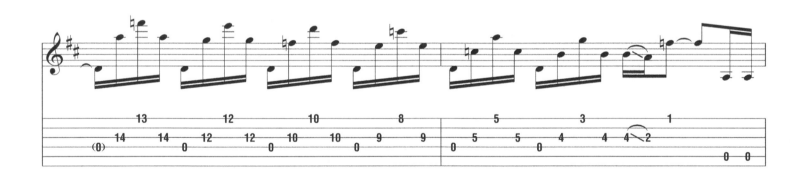

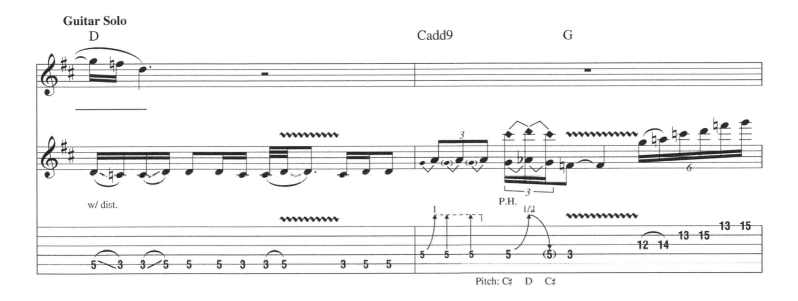

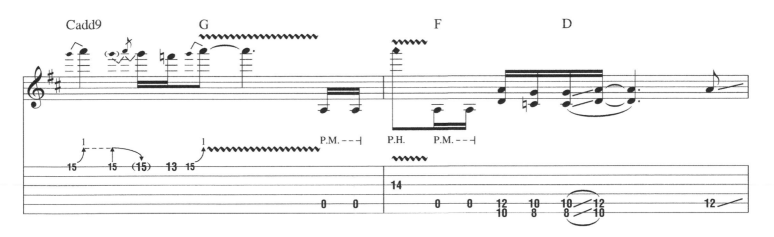

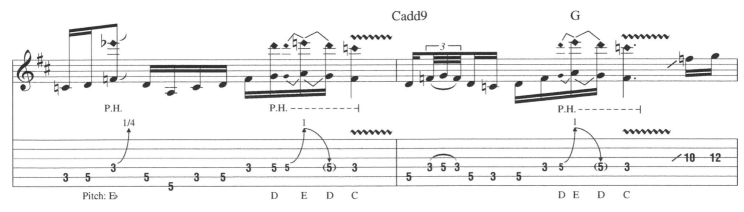

dead   or   a - live, _____   dead   or   a - live. _____

Outro

N.C.(D5)

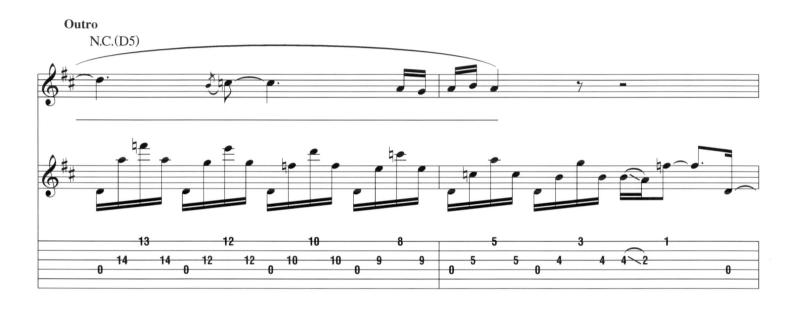

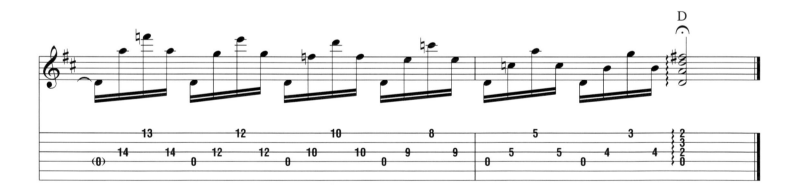

Additional Lyrics

2. Sometimes I sleep, sometimes it's not for days.
   The people I meet always go their sep'rate ways.
   Sometimes you tell the day by the bottle that you drink.
   And times when you're alone, all you do is think.

3. And I walk these streets, a loaded six-string on my back.
   I play for keeps, 'cause I might not make it back.
   I been ev'rywhere, still I'm standing tall.
   I've seen a million faces, and I've rocked them all.

HAL·LEONARD GUITAR PLAY-ALONG

AUDIO ACCESS INCLUDED

This series will help you play your favorite songs quickly and easily. Just follow the tab and listen to the audio to the hear how the guitar should sound, and then play along using the separate backing tracks. Audio files also include software to slow down the tempo without changing pitch. The melody and lyrics are included in the book so that you can sing or simply follow along. **INCLUDES TAB**

VOL. 1 – ROCK	00699570 / $16.99
VOL. 2 – ACOUSTIC	00699569 / $16.99
VOL. 3 – HARD ROCK	00699573 / $17.99
VOL. 4 – POP/ROCK	00699571 / $16.99
VOL. 6 – '90S ROCK	00699572 / $16.99
VOL. 7 – BLUES	00699575 / $17.99
VOL. 8 – ROCK	00699585 / $16.99
VOL. 9 – EASY ACOUSTIC SONGS	00151708 / $16.99
VOL. 10 – ACOUSTIC	00699586 / $16.95
VOL. 11 – EARLY ROCK	00699579 / $14.95
VOL. 12 – POP/ROCK	00699587 / $14.95
VOL. 13 – FOLK ROCK	00699581 / $16.99
VOL. 14 – BLUES ROCK	00699582 / $16.99
VOL. 15 – R&B	00699583 / $16.99
VOL. 16 – JAZZ	00699584 / $15.95
VOL. 17 – COUNTRY	00699588 / $16.99
VOL. 18 – ACOUSTIC ROCK	00699577 / $15.95
VOL. 19 – SOUL	00699578 / $15.99
VOL. 20 – ROCKABILLY	00699580 / $16.99
VOL. 21 – SANTANA	00174525 / $17.99
VOL. 22 – CHRISTMAS	00699600 / $15.99
VOL. 23 – SURF	00699635 / $15.99
VOL. 24 – ERIC CLAPTON	00699649 / $17.99
VOL. 25 – THE BEATLES	00198265 / $17.99
VOL. 26 – ELVIS PRESLEY	00699643 / $16.99
VOL. 27 – DAVID LEE ROTH	00699645 / $16.95
VOL. 28 – GREG KOCH	00699646 / $16.99
VOL. 29 – BOB SEGER	00699647 / $15.99
VOL. 30 – KISS	00699644 / $16.99
VOL. 31 – CHRISTMAS HITS	00699652 / $14.95
VOL. 32 – THE OFFSPRING	00699653 / $14.95
VOL. 33 – ACOUSTIC CLASSICS	00699656 / $17.99
VOL. 34 – CLASSIC ROCK	00699658 / $17.99
VOL. 35 – HAIR METAL	00699660 / $17.99
VOL. 36 – SOUTHERN ROCK	00699661 / $16.95
VOL. 37 – ACOUSTIC UNPLUGGED	00699662 / $22.99
VOL. 38 – BLUES	00699663 / $16.95
VOL. 39 – '80S METAL	00699664 / $16.99
VOL. 40 – INCUBUS	00699668 / $17.95
VOL. 41 – ERIC CLAPTON	00699669 / $17.99
VOL. 42 – COVER BAND HITS	00211597 / $16.99
VOL. 43 – LYNYRD SKYNYRD	00699681 / $17.95
VOL. 44 – JAZZ	00699689 / $16.99
VOL. 45 – TV THEMES	00699718 / $14.95
VOL. 46 – MAINSTREAM ROCK	00699722 / $16.95
VOL. 47 – HENDRIX SMASH HITS	00699723 / $19.99
VOL. 48 – AEROSMITH CLASSICS	00699724 / $17.99
VOL. 49 – STEVIE RAY VAUGHAN	00699725 / $17.99
VOL. 50 – VAN HALEN 1978-1984	00110269 / $17.99
VOL. 51 – ALTERNATIVE '90S	00699727 / $14.99
VOL. 52 – FUNK	00699728 / $15.99
VOL. 53 – DISCO	00699729 / $14.99
VOL. 54 – HEAVY METAL	00699730 / $15.99
VOL. 55 – POP METAL	00699731 / $14.95
VOL. 56 – FOO FIGHTERS	00699749 / $15.99
VOL. 59 – CHET ATKINS	00702347 / $16.99
VOL. 62 – CHRISTMAS CAROLS	00699798 / $12.95
VOL. 63 – CREEDENCE CLEARWATER REVIVAL	00699802 / $16.99
VOL. 64 – THE ULTIMATE OZZY OSBOURNE	00699803 / $17.99
VOL. 66 – THE ROLLING STONES	00699807 / $17.99
VOL. 67 – BLACK SABBATH	00699808 / $16.99

VOL. 68 – PINK FLOYD – DARK SIDE OF THE MOON	00699809 / $16.99
VOL. 69 – ACOUSTIC FAVORITES	00699810 / $16.99
VOL. 70 – OZZY OSBOURNE	00699805 / $16.99
VOL. 73 – BLUESY ROCK	00699829 / $16.99
VOL. 74 – SIMPLE STRUMMING SONGS	00151706 / $19.99
VOL. 75 – TOM PETTY	00699882 / $16.99
VOL. 76 – COUNTRY HITS	00699884 / $14.95
VOL. 77 – BLUEGRASS	00699910 / $15.99
VOL. 78 – NIRVANA	00700132 / $16.99
VOL. 79 – NEIL YOUNG	00700133 / $24.99
VOL. 80 – ACOUSTIC ANTHOLOGY	00700175 / $19.95
VOL. 81 – ROCK ANTHOLOGY	00700176 / $22.99
VOL. 82 – EASY SONGS	00700177 / $14.99
VOL. 83 – THREE CHORD SONGS	00700178 / $16.99
VOL. 84 – STEELY DAN	00700200 / $16.99
VOL. 85 – THE POLICE	00700269 / $16.99
VOL. 86 – BOSTON	00700465 / $16.99
VOL. 87 – ACOUSTIC WOMEN	00700763 / $14.99
VOL. 89 – REGGAE	00700468 / $15.99
VOL. 90 – CLASSICAL POP	00700469 / $14.99
VOL. 91 – BLUES INSTRUMENTALS	00700505 / $15.99
VOL. 92 – EARLY ROCK INSTRUMENTALS	00700506 / $15.99
VOL. 93 – ROCK INSTRUMENTALS	00700507 / $16.99
VOL. 94 – SLOW BLUES	00700508 / $16.99
VOL. 95 – BLUES CLASSICS	00700509 / $15.99
VOL. 96 – BEST COUNTRY HITS	00211615 / $16.99
VOL. 97 – CHRISTMAS CLASSICS	00236542 / $14.99
VOL. 99 – ZZ TOP	00700762 / $16.99
VOL. 100 – B.B. KING	00700466 / $16.99
VOL. 101 – SONGS FOR BEGINNERS	00701917 / $14.99
VOL. 102 – CLASSIC PUNK	00700769 / $14.99
VOL. 103 – SWITCHFOOT	00700773 / $16.99
VOL. 104 – DUANE ALLMAN	00700846 / $16.99
VOL. 105 – LATIN	00700939 / $16.99
VOL. 106 – WEEZER	00700958 / $14.99
VOL. 107 – CREAM	00701069 / $16.99
VOL. 108 – THE WHO	00701053 / $16.99
VOL. 109 – STEVE MILLER	00701054 / $17.99
VOL. 110 – SLIDE GUITAR HITS	00701055 / $16.99
VOL. 111 – JOHN MELLENCAMP	00701056 / $14.99
VOL. 112 – QUEEN	00701052 / $16.99
VOL. 113 – JIM CROCE	00701058 / $16.99
VOL. 114 – BON JOVI	00701060 / $16.99
VOL. 115 – JOHNNY CASH	00701070 / $16.99
VOL. 116 – THE VENTURES	00701124 / $16.99
VOL. 117 – BRAD PAISLEY	00701224 / $16.99
VOL. 118 – ERIC JOHNSON	00701353 / $16.99
VOL. 119 – AC/DC CLASSICS	00701356 / $17.99
VOL. 120 – PROGRESSIVE ROCK	00701457 / $14.99
VOL. 121 – U2	00701508 / $16.99
VOL. 122 – CROSBY, STILLS & NASH	00701610 / $16.99
VOL. 123 – LENNON & MCCARTNEY ACOUSTIC	00701614 / $16.99
VOL. 125 – JEFF BECK	00701687 / $16.99
VOL. 126 – BOB MARLEY	00701701 / $16.99
VOL. 127 – 1970S ROCK	00701739 / $16.99
VOL. 128 – 1960S ROCK	00701740 / $14.99
VOL. 129 – MEGADETH	00701741 / $16.99
VOL. 130 – IRON MAIDEN	00701742 / $17.99
VOL. 131 – 1990S ROCK	00701743 / $14.99
VOL. 132 – COUNTRY ROCK	00701757 / $15.99
VOL. 133 – TAYLOR SWIFT	00701894 / $16.99
VOL. 134 – AVENGED SEVENFOLD	00701906 / $16.99

VOL. 135 – MINOR BLUES	00151350 / $17.99
VOL. 136 – GUITAR THEMES	00701922 / $14.99
VOL. 137 – IRISH TUNES	00701966 / $15.99
VOL. 138 – BLUEGRASS CLASSICS	00701967 / $16.99
VOL. 139 – GARY MOORE	00702370 / $16.99
VOL. 140 – MORE STEVIE RAY VAUGHAN	00702396 / $17.99
VOL. 141 – ACOUSTIC HITS	00702401 / $16.99
VOL. 143 – SLASH	00702425 / $19.99
VOL. 144 – DJANGO REINHARDT	00702531 / $16.99
VOL. 145 – DEF LEPPARD	00702532 / $17.99
VOL. 146 – ROBERT JOHNSON	00702533 / $16.99
VOL. 147 – SIMON & GARFUNKEL	14041591 / $16.99
VOL. 148 – BOB DYLAN	14041592 / $16.99
VOL. 149 – AC/DC HITS	14041593 / $17.99
VOL. 150 – ZAKK WYLDE	02501717 / $16.99
VOL. 151 – J.S. BACH	02501730 / $16.99
VOL. 152 – JOE BONAMASSA	02501751 / $19.99
VOL. 153 – RED HOT CHILI PEPPERS	00702990 / $19.99
VOL. 155 – ERIC CLAPTON – FROM THE ALBUM UNPLUGGED	00703085 / $16.99
VOL. 156 – SLAYER	00703770 / $17.99
VOL. 157 – FLEETWOOD MAC	00101382 / $16.99
VOL. 158 – ULTIMATE CHRISTMAS	00101889 / $14.99
VOL. 159 – WES MONTGOMERY	00102593 / $19.99
VOL. 160 – T-BONE WALKER	00102641 / $16.99
VOL. 161 – THE EAGLES – ACOUSTIC	00102659 / $17.99
VOL. 162 – THE EAGLES HITS	00102667 / $17.99
VOL. 163 – PANTERA	00103036 / $17.99
VOL. 164 – VAN HALEN 1986-1995	00110270 / $17.99
VOL. 165 – GREEN DAY	00210343 / $17.99
VOL. 166 – MODERN BLUES	00700764 / $16.99
VOL. 167 – DREAM THEATER	00111938 / $24.99
VOL. 168 – KISS	00113421 / $16.99
VOL. 169 – TAYLOR SWIFT	00115982 / $16.99
VOL. 170 – THREE DAYS GRACE	00117337 / $16.99
VOL. 171 – JAMES BROWN	00117420 / $16.99
VOL. 172 – THE DOOBIE BROTHERS	00119670 / $16.99
VOL. 173 – TRANS-SIBERIAN ORCHESTRA	00119907 / $19.99
VOL. 174 – SCORPIONS	00122119 / $16.99
VOL. 175 – MICHAEL SCHENKER	00122127 / $16.99
VOL. 176 – BLUES BREAKERS WITH JOHN MAYALL & ERIC CLAPTON	00122132 / $19.99
VOL. 177 – ALBERT KING	00123271 / $16.99
VOL. 178 – JASON MRAZ	00124165 / $17.99
VOL. 179 – RAMONES	00127073 / $16.99
VOL. 180 – BRUNO MARS	00129706 / $16.99
VOL. 181 – JACK JOHNSON	00129854 / $16.99
VOL. 182 – SOUNDGARDEN	00138161 / $17.99
VOL. 183 – BUDDY GUY	00138240 / $17.99
VOL. 184 – KENNY WAYNE SHEPHERD	00138258 / $17.99
VOL. 185 – JOE SATRIANI	00139457 / $17.99
VOL. 186 – GRATEFUL DEAD	00139459 / $17.99
VOL. 187 – JOHN DENVER	00140839 / $17.99
VOL. 188 – MÖTLEY CRUE	00141145 / $17.99
VOL. 189 – JOHN MAYER	00144350 / $17.99
VOL. 191 – PINK FLOYD CLASSICS	00146164 / $17.99
VOL. 192 – JUDAS PRIEST	00151352 / $17.99

Prices, contents, and availability subject to change without notice.

Complete song lists available online.

HAL·LEONARD®

www.halleonard.com

0218

RECORDED VERSIONS®

The Best Note-For-Note Transcriptions Available

AUTHENTIC TRANSCRIPTIONS WITH NOTES AND TABLATURE

14037551 AC/DC – Backtracks	$32.99
00690178 Alice in Chains – Acoustic	$19.99
00694865 Alice in Chains – Dirt	$19.95
00690958 Duane Allman Guitar Anthology	$24.99
00694932 Allman Brothers Band – Volume 1	$24.95
00694933 Allman Brothers Band – Volume 2	$24.95
00694934 Allman Brothers Band – Volume 3	$24.95
00123558 Arctic Monkeys – AM	$22.99
00690609 Audioslave	$19.95
00690820 Avenged Sevenfold – City of Evil	$24.95
00691065 Avenged Sevenfold – Waking the Fallen	$22.99
00123140 The Avett Brothers Guitar Collection	$22.99
00690503 Beach Boys – Very Best of	$19.99
00690489 Beatles – 1	$24.99
00694832 Beatles – For Acoustic Guitar	$22.99
00691014 Beatles Rock Band	$34.99
00694914 Beatles – Rubber Soul	$22.99
00694863 Beatles – Sgt. Pepper's Lonely Hearts Club Band	$22.99
00110193 Beatles – Tomorrow Never Knows	$22.99
00690110 Beatles – White Album (Book 1)	$19.99
00691043 Jeff Beck – Wired	$19.99
00692385 Chuck Berry	$22.99
00690835 Billy Talent	$19.95
00147787 Best of the Black Crowes	$19.99
00690901 Best of Black Sabbath	$19.95
14042759 Black Sabbath – 13	$19.99
00690831 blink-182 – Greatest Hits	$19.95
00148544 Michael Bloomfield Guitar Anthology	$24.99
00158600 Joe Bonamassa – Blues of Desperation	$22.99
00690913 Boston	$19.95
00690491 David Bowie – Best of	$19.99
00690873 Breaking Benjamin – Phobia	$19.95
00141446 Best of Lenny Breau	$19.99
00690451 Jeff Buckley – Collection	$24.95
00690957 Bullet for My Valentine – Scream Aim Fire	$22.99
00691159 The Cars – Complete Greatest Hits	$22.99
00691079 Best of Johnny Cash	$22.99
00690590 Eric Clapton – Anthology	$29.95
00690415 Clapton Chronicles – Best of Eric Clapton	$18.95
00690936 Eric Clapton – Complete Clapton	$29.99
00192383 Eric Clapton – I Still Do*	$19.99
00694869 Eric Clapton – Unplugged	$22.95
00138731 Eric Clapton & Friends – The Breeze	$22.99
00690162 The Clash – Best of	$19.95
00101916 Eric Church – Chief	$22.99
00690828 Coheed & Cambria – Good Apollo I'm Burning Star, IV, Vol. 1: From Fear Through the Eyes of Madness	$19.95
00141704 Jesse Cook – Works Vol. 1	$19.99
00127184 Best of Robert Cray	$19.99
00690819 Creedence Clearwater Revival – Best of	$22.95
00690648 The Very Best of Jim Croce	$19.95
00690613 Crosby, Stills & Nash – Best of	$22.95
00691171 Cry of Love – Brother	$22.99
00690967 Death Cab for Cutie – Narrow Stairs	$22.99
00690289 Deep Purple – Best of	$19.99
00690784 Def Leppard – Best of	$22.99
00692240 Bo Diddley	$19.99
00122443 Dream Theater	$24.99
14041903 Bob Dylan for Guitar Tab	$19.99
00139220 Tommy Emmanuel – Little by Little	$24.99
00691186 Evanescence	$22.99
00691181 Five Finger Death Punch – American Capitalist	$22.99
00690664 Fleetwood Mac – Best of	$19.95
00690870 Flyleaf	$19.95
00691115 Foo Fighters – Wasting Light	$22.99
00690805 Robben Ford – Best of	$22.99
00120220 Robben Ford – Guitar Anthology	$24.99
00694920 Free – Best of	$19.95

00691190 Best of Peter Green	$19.99
00113073 Green Day – ¡Uno!	$21.99
00116846 Green Day – ¡Dos!	$21.99
00118259 Green Day – ¡Tré!	$21.99
00212480 Green Day – Revolutionary Radio*	$19.99
00694854 Buddy Guy – Damn Right, I've Got the Blues	$19.95
00690840 Ben Harper – Both Sides of the Gun	$19.95
00694798 George Harrison – Anthology	$19.95
00690841 Scott Henderson – Blues Guitar Collection	$19.95
00692930 Jimi Hendrix – Are You Experienced?	$24.95
00692931 Jimi Hendrix – Axis: Bold As Love	$22.95
00692932 Jimi Hendrix – Electric Ladyland	$24.95
00690017 Jimi Hendrix – Live at Woodstock	$27.50
00690602 Jimi Hendrix – Smash Hits	$24.99
00119619 Jimi Hendrix – People, Hell and Angels	$22.99
00691152 West Coast Seattle Boy: The Jimi Hendrix Anthology	$29.99
00691332 Jimi Hendrix – Winterland (Highlights)	$22.99
00690793 John Lee Hooker Anthology	$24.99
00121961 Imagine Dragons – Night Visions	$22.99
00690688 Incubus – A Crow Left of the Murder	$19.95
00690790 Iron Maiden Anthology	$24.99
00690684 Jethro Tull – Aqualung	$19.95
00690814 John5 – Songs for Sanity	$19.95
00690751 John5 – Vertigo	$19.95
00122439 Jack Johnson – From Here to Now to You	$22.99
00690271 Robert Johnson – New Transcriptions	$24.99
00699131 Janis Joplin – Best of	$19.95
00690427 Judas Priest – Best of	$22.99
00120814 Killswitch Engage – Disarm the Descent	$22.99
00124869 Albert King with Stevie Ray Vaughan – In Session	$22.99
00694903 Kiss – Best of	$24.95
00690355 Kiss – Destroyer	$16.95
00690834 Lamb of God – Ashes of the Wake	$19.95
00690875 Lamb of God – Sacrament	$19.95
00114563 The Lumineers	$22.99
00690955 Lynyrd Skynyrd – All-Time Greatest Hits	$22.99
00694954 Lynyrd Skynyrd – New Best of	$19.95
00690754 Marilyn Manson – Lest We Forget	$19.95
00694956 Bob Marley – Legend	$19.95
00694945 Bob Marley – Songs of Freedom	$24.95
00139168 Pat Martino – Guitar Anthology	$24.99
00129105 John McLaughlin Guitar Tab Anthology	$24.99
00120080 Don McLean – Songbook	$19.95
00694951 Megadeth – Rust in Peace	$22.95
00691185 Megadeth – Th1rt3en	$22.99
00690505 John Mellencamp – Guitar Collection	$19.95
00209876 Metallica – Hardwired...To Self-Destruct	$22.99
00690646 Pat Metheny – One Quiet Night	$19.95
00690558 Pat Metheny – Trio: 99>00	$24.99
00118836 Pat Metheny – Unity Band	$22.99
00690040 Steve Miller Band – Young Hearts	$19.95
00119338 Ministry Guitar Tab Collection	$24.99
00102591 Wes Montgomery Guitar Anthology	$24.99
00691070 Mumford & Sons – Sigh No More	$22.99
00151195 Muse – Drones	$19.99
00694883 Nirvana – Nevermind	$19.95
00690026 Nirvana – Unplugged in New York	$19.95
00690807 The Offspring – Greatest Hits	$19.95
00694847 Ozzy Osbourne – Best of	$22.95
00690933 Best of Brad Paisley	$22.95
00690995 Brad Paisley – Play: The Guitar Album	$24.99
00694855 Pearl Jam – Ten	$22.99
00690439 A Perfect Circle – Mer De Noms	$19.95
00690499 Tom Petty – Definitive Guitar Collection	$19.99
00121933 Pink Floyd – Acoustic Guitar Collection	$22.99
00690428 Pink Floyd – Dark Side of the Moon	$19.95
00690789 Poison – Best of	$19.99
00694975 Queen – Greatest Hits	$24.95
00690670 Queensryche – Very Best of	$22.99
00109303 Radiohead Guitar Anthology	$24.99
00694910 Rage Against the Machine	$19.95
00119834 Rage Against the Machine – Guitar Anthology	$22.99

00690055 Red Hot Chili Peppers – Blood Sugar Sex Magik	$19.95
00690584 Red Hot Chili Peppers – By the Way	$19.95
00209876 Red Hot Chili Peppers – The Getaway	$22.99
00691166 Red Hot Chili Peppers – I'm with You	$22.99
00690852 Red Hot Chili Peppers – Stadium Arcadium	$24.95
00690511 Django Reinhardt – Definitive Collection	$22.99
14043417 Rodrigo y Gabriela – 9 Dead Alive	$19.99
00690631 Rolling Stones – Guitar Anthology	$27.95
00694976 Rolling Stones – Some Girls	$22.95
00690264 The Rolling Stones – Tattoo You	$19.95
00690685 David Lee Roth – Eat 'Em and Smile	$19.95
00690942 David Lee Roth and the Songs of Van Halen	$19.95
00151826 Royal Blood	$22.99
00174797 Santana – IV*	$22.99
00690031 Santana's Greatest Hits	$19.95
00128870 Matt Schofield Guitar Tab Collection	$22.99
00690566 Scorpions – Best of	$22.95
00690604 Bob Seger – Guitar Collection	$22.99
00138870 Ed Sheeran – X	$19.99
00690803 Kenny Wayne Shepherd Band – Best of	$19.95
00151178 Kenny Wayne Shepherd – Ledbetter Heights (20th Anniversary Edition)	$19.99
00122218 Skillet – Rise	$22.99
00691114 Slash – Guitar Anthology	$24.99
00690813 Slayer – Guitar Collection	$19.99
00120004 Steely Dan – Best of	$24.95
00694921 Steppenwolf – Best of	$22.95
00690655 Mike Stern – Best of	$22.99
00690520 Styx Guitar Collection	$19.95
00120081 Sublime	$19.99
00120122 Sublime – 40oz. to Freedom	$19.95
00690767 Switchfoot – The Beautiful Letdown	$19.95
00690993 Taylor Swift – Fearless	$22.99
00142151 Taylor Swift – 1989	$22.99
00115957 Taylor Swift – Red	$21.99
00690531 System of a Down – Toxicity	$19.95
00694824 James Taylor – Best of	$19.99
00150209 Trans-Siberian Orchestra Guitar Anthology	$19.99
00123862 Trivium – Vengeance Falls	$22.99
00690683 Robin Trower – Bridge of Sighs	$19.95
00660137 Steve Vai – Passion & Warfare	$24.95
00110385 Steve Vai – The Story of Light	$22.99
00690116 Stevie Ray Vaughan – Guitar Collection	$24.95
00660058 Stevie Ray Vaughan – Lightnin' Blues 1983-1987	$27.99
00694835 Stevie Ray Vaughan – The Sky Is Crying	$22.95
00690015 Stevie Ray Vaughan – Texas Flood	$19.99
00183213 Volbeat – Seal the Deal & Let's Boogie*	$19.99
00152161 Doc Watson – Guitar Anthology	$22.99
00690071 Weezer (The Blue Album)	$19.95
00690966 Weezer – (Red Album)	$19.99
00172118 Weezer – (The White Album)*	$19.99
00691941 The Who – Acoustic Guitar Collection	$22.99
00690447 The Who – Best of	$24.95
00122303 Yes Guitar Collection	$22.99
00690916 The Best of Dwight Yoakam	$19.95
00691020 Neil Young – After the Gold Rush	$22.99
00691019 Neil Young – Everybody Knows This Is Nowhere	$19.99
00691021 Neil Young – Harvest Moon	$22.99
00690905 Neil Young – Rust Never Sleeps	$19.99
00690623 Frank Zappa – Over-Nite Sensation	$22.99
00121684 ZZ Top – Early Classics	$24.99
00690589 ZZ Top Guitar Anthology	$24.95

COMPLETE SERIES LIST ONLINE!

HAL•LEONARD®
www.halleonard.com

Prices and availability subject to change without notice.
*Tab transcriptions only.

0917